The SKIER'S COMPANION

The Skier's Companion

CURTIS W. CASEWIT

The Stephen Greene Press
Brattleboro, Vermont
Lexington, Massachusetts

First Edition
Text copyright ©1984 by The Stephen Greene Press

All rights reserved. No part of this book may be reproduced without written permission from the publisher, except by a reviewer who may quote brief passages or reproduce illustrations in a review; nor may any part of this book be reproduced, stored in a retrieval system, or transmitted in any form or by any means electronic, mechanical, photocopying, recording, or other, without written permission from the publisher.

This book is manufactured in the United States of America. It is designed by Irving Perkins Associates and published by The Stephen Greene Press, Fessenden Road, Brattleboro, Vermont 05301.

Library of Congress Cataloging in Publication Data

Casewit, Curtis W.
The skier's companion.

Bibliography: p.
Includes index.
1. Skis and skiing. I. Title.
GV854.C185   1984   796.93   84-18733
ISBN 0-8289-0549-5 (pbk.)

Contents

CHAPTER

	Acknowledgments	viii
ONE	**The Ski Scene: Why You Should Ski (And Why not)**	1

Enthusiasm! The Health Factors. Motivations for Families and Singles. Ski Lodges. "To Dance With Your Soul." The Aesthetics. Why Not to Ski.

TWO	**Beating the Costs of Equipment**	12

Outfitting the New Skier. Buying Skis. Bindings. Ski Boots. Ski Poles. Ski Wear and Extras. Maintenance.

THREE	**Choosing a Ski Area**	26

How the First-Timer Can Find Happiness. Why Ski at the Small Areas. A List for Novices. Ski Area Checklist. For More Information, Write to. . . .

FOUR	**Getting To (And Living Well At) Your Ski Destination**	37

Automobile Travel. Winter Driving. Going By Ski Train. European Trains. Using Buses. Air Carriers. Ski Packages. European Packages. Arranging Your Own U.S. Accommodations. How to Pack for a Ski Vacation.

FIVE	**All About Skiing Inexpensively**	51

Economy Skiing for Average People. The Advantages of Ski Clubs. Special Lift Rates. Real Ski Bumming. Opportunities.

v

SIX	**SKI FITNESS**	58

Some Reasons for Conditioning.　　Before the Season Starts.　　The Gillingham Ski Fitness Test.　　The Complete Skier's Fitness Program.　　Mind Over the Mountain.

SEVEN	**How to Find a Good Ski School**	65

Ski Lessons, Anyone?　　Instruction for the Better Skier.　　How to Evaluate a Ski School.　　What It Takes to Become a Skiing Professional.　　The Cost.　　The Short Ski as a School Tool.　　Teaching Children to Ski.

EIGHT	**Learning to Ski in Record Time**	79

First Steps.　　Climbing, Schussing, Turning.　　The Gliding Wedge.　　Onward, Upward, Downward.　　Advanced Skiing.

NINE	**The ABC's of Ski Lifts and Some Safety Rules**	91

Tramways.　　Gondolas.　　Chairlifts.　　T-Bars.　　Poma Lifts.　　Rope Tows.　　Ski Courtesy (And Some Traffic Rules).　　How Not to Break a Leg. What To Do in Case of a Ski Accident.

TEN	**Interesting North American Ski Resorts**	108

ELEVEN	**Where to Ski in Europe**	128

Why Europe: Some Sound Reasons.　　Travel Tips. Austria and Germany.　　Switzerland.　　France and Italy.

TWELVE	**What Else To Do In Skiland**	149

Cross-Country Skiing.　　Touring Tips.　　Technique.　　One Final X-C Note.　　Ski-Bobbing. Snowshoeing.　　Snowmobiles.　　Avalanches and Other Hazards.

	Bibliography	162

Appendix	**163**
Index	**165**

Acknowledgments

The author would like to thank Curt Chase, Snowmass Ski School Director, and Carl Wilgus, Sun Valley, Idaho, for reading portions of the manuscript. The book would have been less complete without the assistance of ski pioneer Ernie Blake, founder of Taos Ski Valley, and Weems Westfeldt, Ski School Director at Taos, New Mexico. Barbara Roylance and Jim Nelson, supervisors. Winter Park Ski School supported the project. Also helpful were Jan Pilcher of Colorado Ski Country U.S.A.; Gary Tunestead, Idlewild; Dorli Mason, Austrian National Tourist Office; Nancy Overfield, Reno News Bureau; Mike and Pat Gillis of the Beaver's; Karl Boehn; Peaceful Valley Lodge; Jerry Jones and Lillian Ross of the Keystone Resort; and Rainer Kolb, Sun Valley Ski School. For hospitality I thank Hedy Würtz, German National Tourist Office. The input of Dr. H. Roland Zick, National Ski Patrol; Sara Widness, Bolton Valley; Cathy O'Dell-Thompson, Vermont ski publicist; John Gillingham, the Denver Athletic Director; and Mary Ann Limke, greatly enhanced several chapters.

Comments and suggestions from Karen Feldt of the Samsonite Corporation and Richard Crumb of Olin Skis proved valuable. The Swiss National Tourist Office's Willy Isler, Urs Eberhard, and Georges Tauxe were all helpful in Europe. Lastly, my thanks go to Terri Riddell, Crystal Mountain, Washington; Cindy Low, Mt. Bachelor, Oregon; Mike Frome, Professor of Forestry and author in Idaho; Jack Brendlinger, Aspen PR; Peter Fraser, Canada; Paul Brock, journalist and researcher, British Columbia; Cecile Johnson, Ski Artist; Dr. Martin Anderson; Helen Evans, R.N.; and to Niccolo Casewit, John Lane, and Fran Hooker for editorial and research assistance.

C.C.

Denver, Colorado   Autumn 1984

ONE

The Ski Scene: Why You Should Ski (And Why Not)

ENTHUSIASM!

Watch the big Boston ski shops on a late Friday afternoon, the highway to the Sierra resorts early on a Saturday morning, the slopes of Boyne Mountain, Michigan, on a Sunday. Skiers' enthusiasm knows no limits. All over North America skiers clamor for special flights, special trains, airport-to-slope buses, car pools. You can call them "ski nuts," "ski bums," "ski freaks," "ski crazies," or more elegantly, "aficionados."

Business people lend their ears to them and get rich. School principals give them days off from school. At one Colorado area a lodge owner fixed his guests' checkout time at (an early) 9:30 A.M. because the maids wanted to ski. A small midwestern molehill advertised a special ski lift deal from 5:30 A.M. (yes A.M.) to noon, breakfast included, and found plenty of customers for a one-minute run. The devotees turn down high-income positions in the city for a small job related to skiing! Thousands of persons prefer to work in the White Mountains, the Green Mountains, the Blue Mountains, the Rockies, the Sierras.

One teenager had his heart set so much on skiing fast – racing – that he climbed out of a Connecticut window at night, fled from his home, and traveled west to ski. He eventually became a coach and is now a top executive in a ski manufacturing company. He is not alone in his love for skiing. A forest ranger from Pennsylvania packed up his entire family and moved into a Colorado uncertainty because he and his wife wanted to ski. In time he built his own area.

People make remarkable sacrifices for the sake of this winter sport. To spend a day on the slopes, many skiers start traveling as early as 2 A.M., driving through the night. These enthusiasts cover huge distances, so that they can be the first to stand in the lift line.

The appeal of this recreation remains alive. Despite inflation, tight budgets, unemployment, family crises, the army of skiers swells and swells. Once the sport of the Establishment, skiing still fetches the Elite (who rent houses or condominiums at the resorts), but also includes the masses. Everyone seems to manage somehow. Fifteen-year-olds work all summer, so that they can ski in winter. Retired couples move from Kansas to Utah, so that they can enjoy the powder snow. Chicagoans save all year for a single week in Sugarbush, Vermont. The pendulum has swung from the former sport of the Social Lion – and male domain – to women and family.

Ski areas and resorts are now catering to families. These days no operator would dare to be caught without a nursery. Here you can leave youngsters of various ages – even 3-year-olds – for a day of skiing. While you're on the slopes, the children are supplied with toys, hot chocolate, and often lunch or a nurse to change diapers. (At a small California weekend spot, the nursery is even owned and supervised by a physician and his wife, an RN.) Genuine family interest also extends to many resorts. In Vermont, for instance, one nursery is set up to feed and diaper one-month-old babies while the parents enjoy the outdoors. In "Preschools-Ski-Schools" the tots play ski games and engage in kiddies' races. Resorts also gear special children's ski classes for the youngest on tiny hills. And after supper at the lodge your youngster can disappear into the "game room," where a few coins will activate video games and other amusements. Ping-pong, pool, and movies are available. Besides, skiing today comes with all the creature comforts. Some vacationers opt for deluxe hotels like the Keystone (Colorado) Lodge or the Westin in Vail. Modern areas boast large warming houses at the base of their slopes. Up-to-date lifts are padded. Contemporary ski togs (more later) protect you from wind and snow. All this ensures the family's comfort.

Current ski techniques require little physical strength, and shorter skis allow you to learn much in a few hours. Skiing is even taught to those who are blind and those who are legless. And for all, snowmaking guarantees a good white cover.

Larger ski companies also offer activities for those who prefer to toboggan or skate or take a sleigh ride. (See Chapter 12 on cross-country skiing, ski-bobbing, and snowshoeing.)

Nature still survives in the flatlands, on the hillsides, and especially in the high Rockies. Ski on a weekday, and you'll find solitude among snow-laden Engleman spruce, lodgepole pines, Douglas firs, all with their untouched white pillows. The sky can be as grey as lead, then suddenly change to aquamarine. You stop: a hawk circles overhead, a lonely falcon swoops, a black raven set-

Finding quiet is one motivation of the harried city dweller. (McCullough, Taos Ski Valley, NM)

tles on a boulder. Up on Aspen Mountain, the jays wait to be fed by lunching skiers. Down in the Wyoming valleys, white trumpeter swans mingle on ponds with wild ducks. You are one with the season and the land.

Adults who normally inhabit the city's concrete, steel, and glass jungles or the relentless sameness of suburbs, especially appreciate Snow Country. The skier's white outdoors erases all pressures and worries. This feeling of freedom and the liberation from the work world is well expressed in the simple song of the National Ski Patrol. A few lines: "The Sun is Bright; The Snow is white; And nothing is in between; All the busy life I knew has left my mind."

This is all true, especially if you choose ski areas wisely for their remoteness, or if you can come at the beginning and end of the peak season. You may arrive out of sorts, depressed, or simply tired. An hour on skis often suffices for some old skiers; they're seized by a giddy and euphoric sensation akin to a religious experience.

THE HEALTH FACTORS

An hour on skis can magically bring out your well-being. Whether you're an expert or a beginner, on thin cross-country "Skinnies" or wide Alpine skis, you'll inevitably leave behind your daily concerns. Instead, you will be involved with the task at hand – to learn to ski, or to ski better, or, if you're in motion, to pick your route down a hillside or mountain.

Why is this sport such an Rx for health? It tones up your entire system. Your legs, arms, shoulders, and back are all in motion. Every muscle is stimulated, and the joints are limbered up. The heart is forced to pump more blood, which improves circulation. The bracing air activates the oxygen-starved lungs. (Smoking is almost impossible while you ski.) Cardiologists and physical fitness experts have long recommended this activity for all ages. If it is sunny, your body gets Vitamin D through the skin; and even in a snowstorm, the liver, the bile, the stomach, the glands get a good workout. Your blood pressure is lowered. Like a hardy walk, the run on skis rejuvenates the entire human being. After downhill or cross-country skiing for a few hours, you think faster and feel better. In the evening, thirst vies with hunger. Drink and food seldom tasted this good. A few days on the slopes dissolves stress.

The health factors are so proven that one life insurance company has enrolled members of several ski clubs up to the age of 55 at an extra low rate and without medical examination. One insurance administrator explains his firm's philosophy this way: "We believe skiers are healthier and live longer than their more sedentary friends." That is one reason why older (ages 55 to 75) folks still hit the slopes.

This winter sport – especially in cold weather – consumes calories and thus helps some people reduce. Beginners, hard-core skiers, or racers naturally get a better workout on the slopes. Compared with other activities, skiing burns up a considerable number of you-know-what. Here's a comparison table for 60 minutes of:

Desk sitting: 20 calories
Standing at a drafting board: 30 calories
Hiking in flat country: 130 to 150 calories
Hiking uphill: 200 calories
Cycling: 200 to 300 calories
Skiing: *500 to 900 calories!*

MOTIVATIONS FOR FAMILIES AND SINGLES

Why do you ski? Ask ten people and you may get ten answers. An important one has to do with human values. Skiing gives self-confidence, bolsters your ego, and stills the visual appetites of would-be painters. The slopes are "where it's at" in the eighties. The sport builds an easy camaraderie between singles or couples. The ski fields are democratic: Royalty mingles here with blue collar workers, and every ethnic extraction can play. You can talk to anyone on the slopes and lifts. A Colorado psychologist claims special family benefits as well, and the theory that "the family who skis together stays together" does make some sense. Preventive against divorce? Sanity restorer? All possible.

For singles, the lure is often companionship and sex. Some time ago, advertisements by one Vermont resort promised "The Sensuous Vacation": "We don't know what turns you on. But if you love life, and people, the outdoors and a good time, skiing is one of the things you'll have to experience at least once. Which brings us to your vacation . . ."

For many years, a famous Colorado ski spa showed a circle of lovey-dovey singles at "The Total Ski Resort." A seductive color brochure by the High Sierra Winter Sports Association asked us for years to "tumble out to virgin morning snow." At night, we could "sit in the hearth blaze, wiggling toes," and most important, "get into the swing with Ladyluck."

There were always erotic overtones in ski advertising. Four scantily dressed females and a solitary pair of skis assured us that, "Duofold makes warm-blooded girls . . ." Manipulating the touchstones of desire, the copywriters used the words "skin" . . . "body moisture" . . . "playing" . . . with virtuosity.

It is true that some single men and women patronize winter sports towns mainly because they search for sex. A book for novices states that "everyone looks so much more handsome on the slopes," and that "acquaintances come easy."

They do. Chairlifts, which take the skier up the mountain, are built for two or three. ("It's much warmer," a consultant told ski area executives not long ago, asking them to forget about the old-fashioned uphill conveyances that seat only *one* person.) A Michigan area – and others around the country – went further: they installed chairs seating four people. Ski lodges do their share, too. As humorist Morten Lund puts it: "The lodge is the place wherein much aprés-ski activity is proposed and some occasionally consumated, facilitated by interconnected balconies and shared bathrooms . . ."

SKI LODGES

Ski resorts all come with lodges that have fireplaces for cozy *tête-à-têtes*. This business is so important that one new western area almost went bankrupt because it could offer only a few motels instead of lodges. "Nobody could get acquainted," the area manager complained. "So nobody came." Solution: a big ski hostelry with a fireplace.

The ambience and versatility of the ski hostelry should not be underestimated. Ski lodges can be everything to everyone: mountain retreat, meeting ground, mating ground. In the classic lodges, the owners know their flock, even by name. A genuine ski lodge serves food, and the best ones do so on long sit-together tables. The ideal places draw a lot of unattached people, who can thus get to know one another on the premises. With the affluence of the eighties for some people, there is a trend toward variety and luxury. You can find ski lodges with superb Austrian chefs (Liftline Lodge, Stratton Mountain, Vermont), wine stewards (Squaw Valley Lodge), bellhops in dark-blue blazers (Keystone Lodge), nightclubs (Heavenly Valley, California), elevators (Jackson, Wyoming), and ankle-deep carpets (Beaver's, Winter Park, Colorado). Swiss maitre d's, imported champagne for honeymooners, color television, deluxe private baths, whirlpools, fancy telephones, and automatic bowling equipment are not extraordinary extras, and every manager hopes to install a Finnish sauna and a teakwood hot tub.

At the "Beaver's Village" in Winter Park, Colorado, the charisma becomes clearest of all. You begin to take the fireplaces for granted, of course, and you expect to be seated for dinner with interesting people. For years, this lodge built its reputation with an Indonesian chef, who laid out an actual *Rijsttafel* for the astonished midwesterners. After supper, the guests are encouraged to try a short moonlight excursion on cross-country skis. What a good life! Trimmings like these make the sport even more inviting.

Some lodges, notably in California, New Mexico, Utah, and Vermont, offer more than just comfort, companionship, and joie de vivre. Several winter places cater to particular kinds of people, such as intellectuals in quest of other intellectuals (who just happen to ski). Executives in search of business contacts, urbanites in search of the outdoors, and super skiers keen on ski equipment make up the rest.

The old lodges at Alta, Utah, deserve special note, for they radiate a unique warmth. Guests eat together, and because there are no taverns, there is no place to go at night other than to lived-in couches and chairs for long talks or reading. The lack of nightclub dancing brings an older, often married, group of people to these Utah enclaves: west and east coast publishers and editors, scientists, Ph.D.'s, specialized teachers, and so on.

Skiing is indeed a congenial sport. Upon request, strangers help each other on the slopes. If you fall and need help, someone gives you a hand. Ski classes bring quick acquaintances. Conversation flows easily in the lift line.

"TO DANCE WITH YOUR SOUL"

Skiers' reactions are almost Pavlovian. The veteran begins to get stirred up as he approaches a mountain. He then steps into his bindings. The moment he pushes off and darts downhill over the snow, he feels light and alert and somehow born anew. He is in a new orbit. Speed and the adrenalin rush have something to do with it, especially for better skiers. But even the slowest feel *the motion*. Nothing else counts in their minds just then but to move, to come down the hill through sun and wind. A poetic airline publicist wrote about it all with unexpected eloquence. "What is skiing? Skiing is to dance with your soul!"

The exhilaration has been described by the world's great authors, too. Thomas Mann, in "Magic Mountain," compares the skier's downhill journey to "the rise and fall of a ship on a billowy sea." Hemingway spoke of a "floating, flying, marvellously dropping sensation." Novelist Irwin Shaw, an avid

The Ski Scene **7**

skier, always couched his thoughts in the right words. "The love of speed is seated deep among the primal instincts of mankind," he says, and adds, "Skiing gives the fullest play to that instinct." Switzerland-based novelist Shaw has also commented on the "sober joy, especially keen for the city man, of merely breathing deeply of the cold winter air, and looking around." Some of our more sensitive musicians – Leonard Bernstein is one example – continue to show up on the slopes.

Skiing means facing the primitive forces of nature and turning back the clock to the days when there were no cars, no motor bikes, and few trains. Some skiers indulge in fantasies of the American West in the 1850s, of hardy, blizzard-fighting people like Snowshoe Thompson; others transform their dreams into reality. These people shun the groomed trails and go exploring the glades, bowls, and steep chutes of the natural (and often untouched) terrain on a mountain.

THE AESTHETICS

Liberation from the routine self then. There is only the moment, the present, the experience. Another world. The challenge of nature. Our basic desire for beauty, our thirst for color.

Scenery like this alp is a magnet too. (Warren Miller)

The skier stands amid the stunning scenery. (British Columbia Tourism)

The Ski Scene

The most humble ski area can present a pretty picture of the undulating terrain, the possibility of higher mountains, the snow-bordered tree branches. You see people on the chairlift; the underside of their laminated fiberglass wonders are stark yellow or green, even tulip red. Black skis contrast with the morning sky. Bright orange, egg-yellow, and even purple skis appear. Clothes also dazzle the eyes. Parkas come with cheery patterns, and multicolored or candy-striped pants look smart. (You also notice people in blue jeans and some in farmer's overalls.) The faces shine.

Now you are being wafted upward, over the picturesque lodge and condo roofs. Ski poles glint in the sun. You start off: If there is a fresh layer of snow, a white feather follows in your wake. You're deposited on the mountain top. Your eyes take in surrounding crests, a landscape that ebbs and flows. The Rockies stand sharply etched against the whiteness. One can absorb the scenery alone, or in company. The good skier has the advantage of savoring high mountains in their primitive winter state. He or she can go to less accessible places, away from the crowds, to ferret out large untouched snowfields, with all their hues of blue and all the right mauve shadows. The *clean*, white environment of this sport is unrivaled.

Paul Ramlow, an Idaho instructor, taught, watched, and questioned hundreds of skiers for many years. His survey categorized why people decide to take up the sport:

They have leisure time.
They have money.
They like to wear ski clothes.
It's a sport in which they compete against themselves.
They can do it alone.
They meet new people.
They can find sex partners.
They like to buy equipment (the shopping instinct).
It builds their ego.
They get an aesthetic satisfaction.
It gives them a reason to be outdoors.
It exercises their muscles.
They do it to please someone else.
They can do as though they were skiers and enjoy the aprés-ski life instead.

WHY NOT TO SKI

Included with the joys of skiing are some negative aspects.

Unless you watch out and cut corners, skiing can be extremely expensive. A New Jersey family of four may spend as much as $3,000 for a deluxe week at a major western resort (travel included). Equipment can be prohibitive: $350

Even older people, like this well-known ski area operator, can take part. (Gallard, Taos Ski Valley, NM)

skis, $300 boots, $150 bindings. Clothes can carry outrageous price tags. Accommodations further your expenses – $155-per-night condo (for two) is common, with $50 for dinner *a deux*. Watch these prices soar by the year 2000!

Skiing is more dangerous than staying in bed; Hannes Schneider, one of the European pioneers, used to say that you only had to ski for 1000 days to reap your leg fracture. Broken arms, injured knees, punctured lungs, brain concussions, near suffocations in avalanches, saber-like skin slicing, and snow-blindness are remote possibilities. Novelist Irwin Shaw has torn all the ligaments in his shoulders and claims 18 stitches in his skin. Ski celebrity Stein Eriksen tore his Achilles tendon. (The author of this book was himself on crutches for nearly a year after suffering a "comminuted" fracture of tibia and fibula.) You can wind up with a sprain, frostbite, or if the chairlift stops for two hours and you're to be evacuated by rope, with a phobia of high lifts.

Add to this picture the long expensive drives to a far-away ski resort, often under impossible blizzard and road conditions. Skiers complain about cold temperatures, overpriced lift tickets, and traffic jams en route home, where the checking account may now be overdrawn. (After all, skiing is a $1 billion industry.)

The sport demands some fitness, and about 20% of the first-timers don't come back after the first day.

One-time TV personality Pat O'Connor often regaled his audiences with long masochistic descriptions of the skier's woes. Among them: 1) His drive may take from six to sixteen hours, depending on the weather (which will be bad). 2) His feet hurt all the time. 3) Upon his arrival, he finds out what skiing is all about: "You wait in line to buy your lift ticket. You wait in line to buy your ski school ticket, you wait in line for the lifts, and you wait in line for lunch. There is a rumor that they're going to start a new ski area in Vermont with no skiing, just lines. In France, you not only stand in line, but someone also stands on your $300 skis."

This book tells you how to avoid the pitfalls and plights of skiing. You'll learn how to cut your expenses and at the same time increase the pleasures of skiing and living.

TWO

Beating The Costs Of Equipment

OUTFITTING THE NEW SKIER

Ski equipment is expensive, and if you're an average wage earner, you'll try to shave costs for both grownups and children. Can it be done? Just ask the "ski bum" who spends entire winters on his/her skis. Expense-paring systems may be adopted by families, too.

First of all, if you've never skied, try the sport with rental equipment. The same suggestion makes sense if you plan to ski just once a year on vacation. Even for two weeks, it is cheaper and more practical to rent skis, boots, and poles. (Almost no shop rents sportswear, however; you will need your own parka and stretch pants.)

Visit the ski shop on a weekday, if possible. Avoid peak periods so that you get enough attention. In general, the big city sports emporiums charge less than rental shops at the large resorts. If you fly, however, the convenience of the local rental service makes sense. The average American all-inclusive daily rental costs about as much as an average ski restaurant dinner, say fifteen dollars. For the whole week, equipment rates go down of course. (You can also get your gear by the season.) Later, if you ski regularly, you will probably want to own your own equipment. One advantage: you will know the performance of your own skis and bindings, which are generally better than the heavily used rentals.

Some people do not bother with lift skiing because it requires the more costly synthetic Alpine skis and the heavy plastic boots. Instead, these new skiers avoid the uphill machinery altogether and go on cross-country tours instead, using "skinny" cross-country skis and simple bindings. The boots are much lighter and less expensive than their Alpine counterparts. In total, touring equip-

Historic photo shows some skiers' sentiments about high prices. (Mt. Mansfield Co., Stowe, VT)

ment costs only a fraction of the heavier downhill items. Cross-country skis can also be *rented* at many shops. (For more details on cross-country skiing, see Chapter 12 and the Bibliography at the end of this book.)

Renting Alpine or X-C equipment certainly makes sense for a week's skiing in Europe. On both sides of the Atlantic, beginners need only *rent* – and not buy – their first short-short ATM (American Teaching Method) skis; most people later graduate to a greater length.

There's another angle for novice skiers. They can buy whole outfits at special prices. Commercially minded mass merchandizers often advertise skis, bindings, boots, and poles for a total package price.

Some dollars can also be shaved by looking for slightly used skis and poles. How does the beginner know if the used stuff is worth the money? You can be pretty sure if you stick to a small specialty ski shop. The owners know equipment. Likewise, you can find bargains at the yearly ski swap of the National Ski Patrol. Some patrollers are always on hand for advice. One clue is price. Used skis should be at least 25 percent less than their original retail cost. If the gear is extra cheap, be aware – you may get a lemon. Check skis for slashes and scrapes on the metal edges and plastic bottoms; inspect the full length of the skis for cracks. A novice can also go to a shop or check out a Sunday ad with an experienced skier who will tell at a glance if the skis have enough "life" left. Used equipment can be fine for the beginner who patronizes a reliable store.

Another approach to savings? In the United States, the end of the season is always best for a buying spree. Every type of ski equipment can then be had at every kind of outlet for 25 to 55 percent off. (Don't count on discounts in Europe, though. European retailers generally hold on to their merchandise for the following season.)

Not all skiers want to tie up savings during the summer months, and the selection isn't wide in March or April. Another tactic is to make the rounds of several outlets, including discount stores and department stores. Watch the advertisements in the newspapers for sales promotions of large sporting goods dealers in your area. Avoid buying new ski gear at the posh resorts; at some of them, the retailers not only get their full markup but add another 20 percent to the city retail price.

BUYING SKIS

A humorist once observed that his friends all flocked to Sugarbush, Vermont. They really didn't like to ski. "They were in it for the equipment." The barb packs some truth because the gear, with its variety and complexity, can be fascinating to gadget-conscious people. Especially skis.

It may be a good idea to head for a specialized sporting goods store or a specialty ski shop and ask someone to help you with your first purchase. The

Beating the Costs of Equipment

salesperson may ask for your height (or judge it), for your weight (or estimate it), and about your skiing ability (be honest). You'll be asked how often the skis will be used and how much is to be spent. First-rate shops are adept at matching the customer with the appropriate equipment. They will not sell a novice a pair of high-performance skis, for instance.

Whether addressing a beginner or an expert, a good salesperson will avoid too much technical jargon and speak simply, without the buzz words that are for hot doggers, Olympians or the trade itself. If a salesman tells you, like this manufacturer to a *Ski Business* audience, "We will be using our HPG base, a high molecular weight sintered material, and a four-step Diamond Glide tuning process. This bevels the ski's extremities at the tip and tail, deburs the edge," then you better try another shop!

Must the first-season skier plunk down a little or a lot? Two theories: Some people start with an inexpensive pair and move up to more costly fiberglass during the following year; other individuals begin with the best name brand models, which last a long time and usually ski with winged, inspiring ease. A compromise often works best.

Buy a lesser-known label of sandwich construction skis. These can be almost as good as the famous ones, "obeying" when you order them to steer left and "forgiving" mistakes. Small children can do quite well on cheap wooden skis. Plastic boards are also available for tots; the bindings work with most snow boots. Buy skis *slightly* longer than the child, keeping in mind a youngster's growth; the skis should last through at least one more winter. It's foolish to spend a great deal for the beginning child. Consider a ski package with all the items included at one price.

What about sizes? For the beginning adult, a short ski is easier to handle than a long one. Indeed, short skis are popular; long ones serve only stronger skiers and downhill racers. For the first few lessons on rented (or bought) equipment, the American Teaching Method (ATM) recommends 130 to 140 cm skis for ladies and 150-160 cms for men. Many novices quickly understand the convenience of shorter skis; they're so much easier to learn on. The short-short wide GLM (Graduated Length Method) – a product of the sixties and seventies – is no longer found at many ski areas. Basically, the heavier a person and the better the skier, the longer the skis.

How about the intermediate? Men will sometimes move on to lengths varying from 170 to 205 cms. For ladies the range is 150 to 180. As an intermediate, you'll appreciate turning and tracking qualities. (Tracking means holding a course or a line.) The ski should work *for* the skier, not against him. If in doubt, shorter is better unless you plan to ski very fast.

When going into a shop, the beginner can perform a simple test by putting two running surfaces together and pressing. The skis should bounce back with ease. If they have no spring or flex and feel too stiff, they're wrong for the novice. An additional pointer: skis for beginners are generally *lighter* than those used by advanced recreational skiers or racers.

Where to buy? In department stores, the personnel are often switched from selling buttons and scissors to selling winter sports items, and some sales people in large sporting goods stores only know rifles and fishing gear. On the other hand, specialty ski outlets employ *skiers,* who can be trusted. Unfortunately, the merchandise will usually cost more there.

At this point you should also know a bit more about materials. Fiberglass usually consists of several layers of glass fibers bonded to plastic or of natural epoxy resins bonded to a wood core. Technology has advanced since the fifties when the epoxy skis first showed up. Some prototypes wore out quickly. By contrast, certain plastics combinations are now so rugged that they're practically indestructible. Engineering has played a part in the development, along with research on behalf of downhill and slalom racers. The recreational skier of the eighties, therefore, gets a much better product than that of 20 years ago.

A cross-section of a ski reveals aluminum alloys, fine woods, rubber, fiberglass laminations, plastics, and steel. The manufacturer's experience comes into play here. Better skiers demand better performance and hence more sophisticated equipment. One typical brand for longtime skiers, for example, uses epoxy-impregnated fiberglass and a high density foam core instead of wood. Other manufacturers insist on wood cores. Whatever their composition, these modern winter sports products absorb shock with great ease and eliminate vibrations.

Certain expensive skis are often status symbols. Manufacturers make no bones about this. An ad for one brand came right out and showed a Rolls Royce. "Let's face it," the ad began. "Our skis do great things for the owner's ego. Will owning a Rolls make you a better driver? Not necessarily. But owning a pair of X-skis will make you a better skier." While this is true for everyone except the rank beginner, it's also true that you appear as a wealthier – and more substantial – person with the right brand. You need only look around when you ride up the lifts from St. Moritz or Gstaad: you see sleek $300-and-up skis with carefully chosen names like "Atomic," "Dynamic," "Blizzard," and "Lightning Bold."

Another twist to the ski-as-status symbol game revolves around the racing circuit. An Olympic or World Cup victory by a racer inevitably means increased revenues for the sponsoring ski company. The racers not only do their part by winning, they also make a point to conspicuously display the undersides of their skis, revealing name-brands to the television camers at the finish lines!

The status of a ski is not as important as the quality and the guarantee behind that quality. If you intend to ski much, the guarantee is important. Indeed, a quality product can be judged by what the manufacturer will do about breakage and major defects. Most firms, especially the well-known ones, unconditionally guarantee their sporting goods against any factory defect. The warranty period is usually one year. If you can't get a written assurance, you may be better off to switch to another brand.

Beating the Costs of Equipment **17**

Even to the experts, a ski is a complicated thing indeed. There are a number of functional differences, and engineers become enthusiastic about them all: length, weight, surface contact length, height and dimensions of the roll back section of the ski tips, the running surface groove, the width in various sections, the thickness, the camber, flex factor, torsion factor, damping factor, and finally, the polar moment factor.

Factories go to incredible lengths to test their products. In Austria, for instance, a ski maker cooked up a testing apparatus that can inflict 5,000 vibrations in one hour to a fiberglass board. Most ski factories use computers for testing.

BINDINGS

Bindings are sold separately from skis, and then mounted, hopefully, by an expert. Quality is essential in this item. Indeed, bindings may well be your most important acquisition. Reason: your safety. An inferior product causes broken legs. Some bindings don't have enough release angles. Some contraptions are too lightly and "tinnily" built, with important parts at the mercy of cold temperatures. Specialty shops favor a solid type, such as the Look, which

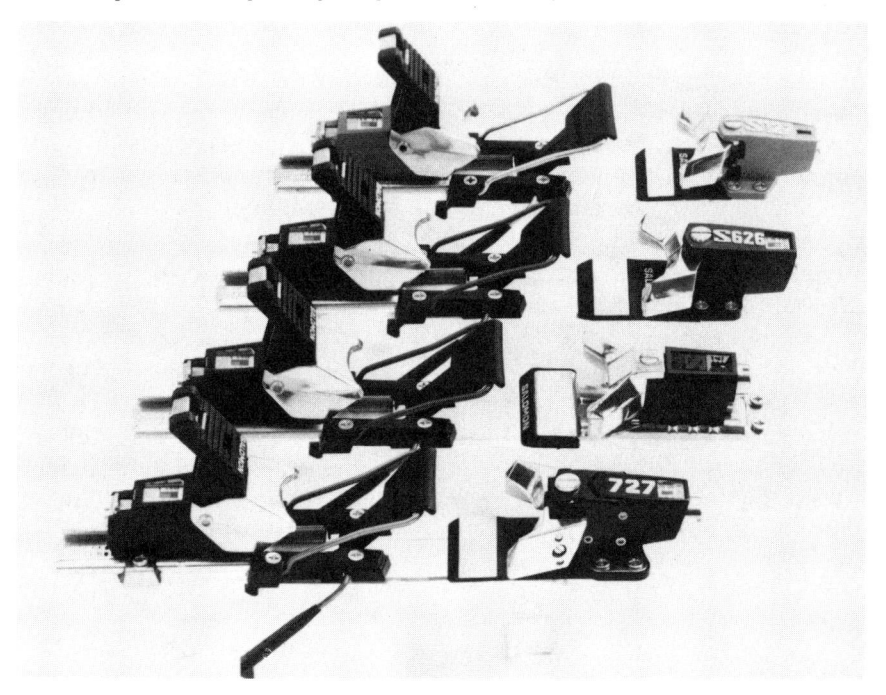

Sleek, modern bindings like these cost a great deal of money, but they're safe if properly adjusted. (Salomon)

allows you to step in with ease. (One easy "click" does it.) This classic binding has a turnable heel, a sensor toe, and sealed mechanisms. It is so well made that it lasts for years. Likewise, Salomon bindings are respected for craftsmanship and reliability.

Some makes of bindings require the knowledge of an engineer and the contortion ability of a Yogi. These are not for the average skier. Beginners particularly should beware of not buying an overly complicated product. More parts can freeze and malfunction. Good bindings fetch a high price. An adult should count on making an investment from $60 to $180.

Children once had to content themselves with an adult's version, but they now have their own. Various makes are available, all designed for a youngster's smaller weight.

A word of caution. A new skier shouldn't leave the store until he or she understands the workings of the binding. The salesperson ought to be able to explain how you get in and out of it, and how the mechanism should be adjusted to make it release in case of a fall. Some buyers don't bother to ask; others hit the slopes without listening. Ironically, a few beginners can't remember how to get back into their skis, and have to ask a ski patroller for instructions. (Likewise, this author, while on a trip to Switzerland, was unable to *get off* the skis because of an over-complex binding.)

Use a competent ski shop to mount your bindings; the latter will probably malfunction if improperly installed. Likewise, you should take your skis periodically to a skilled mechanic to test and adjust the bindings. This becomes especially important for air travelers, whose bagged equipment gets indelicate treatment from airport workers. A long cold automobile trip or several days of actual skiing also dictate a binding check. A friend of this ski writer forgot to check out her bindings at the beginning of a new season. Result: she came out of one ski and fell on her shoulder with dire consequences. (For more details on avoiding accidents, read Chapter 9.)

Your new pair of skis should come with a "ski brake," which is attached to the binding. If you fall, the brake lives up to its name: it prevents your skis from careening downhill on their own steam. The brakes also fulfill a second purpose – they help tie your skis together for easier shouldering en route to the hill. Pot-bellied old-timers who formerly had to bend down to fasten antiquated straps around their lower feet are now free to simply step onto their skis. The brake automatically comes up until the first fall or a return to the base lodge.

SKI BOOTS

Ski boots are the most individual and tricky part of your equipment. Your feet may ache unless you get a perfect fit. And without a perfect fit you won't be able to transmit your ankle motions to your skis and have adequate control

Some ski areas help you test your ski bindings. (Attitash Mountain, NH)

of your edges. Remember to try boots on in your ski socks. Boots should be snug, but not tight, and there should not be painful pressure anywhere.

You can purchase boots for narrow, medium, and wide feet, and because of anatomical differences, there are special boots for women. The side of the boot must always offer support. A skier ought to feel this hold, which is an acceptable tightness. If boots feel too comfortable, they may become too loose after a few ski trips. On the other hand, the toes can have some freedom, or the circulation will be cut off, resulting in cold feet. Once the boot is buckled, it should be especially snug (but painlessly so) at the arch.

One important rule: *The heel should have no play.* That's why a boot salesperson usually makes you kick your heel against the floor. Standing up and leaning forward is one good test. Does the heel wiggle inside your boot? Then it doesn't fit. Now start walking. Your steps will feel as awkward as a diver's. Ski boots have become taller and heavier. But your feet should not hurt.

If you plan to ski every weekend all winter, you'll be ahead by going for a higher price range.

As a novice skier, you shouldn't let a sales clerk talk you into buying the first pair you're trying on. A clerk's impatience is a sure sign of an inferior store because no first-rate merchant is in a hurry to get rid of unsuitable merchandise. The quality operator wants a satisfied customer who comes back, so choose a *patient* salesperson for this important purchase. (One way to get better service: avoid shopping at rush hours, on Saturdays, or holidays.) There is nothing wrong with trying on five pairs, or even more. If none of them work, the skier should take his or her business elsewhere. Rather than selling you the wrong boots, the quality store won't object if you walk out.

Keep in mind that brand names are unimportant for the average person; only the fit matters. Sometimes, the unknown make works better than the most advertised wonder boots.

Most ski boots consist of a hard outer shell plus an inside liner which can be leather, cotton, or synthetics. Some models feature a three-piece construction.

A perfect fit is achieved in expensive models by means of introducing liquid foam or putty into an inner "bladder." The heated foam conforms to the foot, which increases comfort if you have an unusual foot shape. On the exterior of the boot, the buckles have become easier on your fingers. And space-age possibilities include boots that open in the rear. The rear-entry system eliminates the series of buckles that can cause undue pressure on the foot and ankle and also reduces the bulk and weight of the boot. Some experts claim that rear-entry boots can provide a better fit and are easier to put on. Their breakthrough came during the early eighties.

This modern plastic article, unlike the old leather boot, enjoys a long life. The strong new synthetics do not break down or change their shape. On the other foot, the more complicated a product, the more that can go wrong with it.

Beating the Costs of Equipment

Footwear for intermediates, expert skiers, and racers, is a little stiffer than that for the novice. All boots reach over the shins, giving super-control on the slopes.

How much should you spend? Boots range from $80 to $500 and $200 or so buys a good pair.

Sometimes it can be confusing to choose the right boot because of the price. Consumers have a tendency to equate price with quality, but when choosing ski boots it helps to know what you're getting for your money. Shell materials vary in cost depending on the complexity of the plastic which determines the boot flexibility. The inner boot materials that keep your feet warm and guard against abrasion and shock also vary. The less expensive product may feel cushiony or foamy. The more expensive item will feel firm, but after about ten minutes will soften up and conform to your foot.

One final note: the skier's footwear is now made in lively colors, including firehouse red and tulip yellow. Whatever their color, boots are a crucial item and an important factor in your skiing equipment. Choose wisely!

SKI POLES

Unless you're a racer, don't worry too much about brand names or ad claims. Most poles are made of aluminum alloys. These materials are light, yet strong. Pole baskets should be small; the most costly ones are made of a metal ring held by rubber spokes. (Plastics are popular.)

The best poles fit the human hand fairly accurately; they're one piece so they can be flicked with a minimum of effort. Expensive poles often have adjustable straps, complete with buckles. First-rate poles are extremely light. Lengths used to be decided by letting you hold a pole vertically. In the old days if it reached just under your shoulders, it was the correct size. Today, the skier uses much shorter ski poles, i.e., about hip length. Too long a pole throws you backward, a situation to be avoided. Too short a pole gives your turns little support; you stab the air instead of the snow.

Children also need the right size of pole for the proper pole "plant" in the snow and, ultimately, ski control. To judge size, turn the pole upside down and grasp the pointed end above the pole basket. If the youngster's elbow is comfortably bent without having to reach too high or low in front, then the poles are perfect. If not, then it's time for a new pair.

SKI WEAR AND EXTRAS

To numerous people of both sexes, skiing exerts a special charm because they can dress smartly. Up-to-date ski wear enhances a man's looks and makes some women irresistible. The colors of shirts, parkas, sweaters, and pants become more dazzling every season. Each year brings new hues, new materials, and new flattering, slimming ski wear. Should you follow the trends? Perhaps so, if you're status-conscious, in the public limelight, or normally someone who always dresses in the latest fashions. Elegant resorts like Vail, Colorado; Sugarbush or Stratton, Vermont; and Deer Valley, Utah, justly conjure up pictures of well-garbed skiers, those who choose to engage in the dazzling display of pants and parkas.

Ski wear gives you another chance to evaluate a good store. Do they carry a real selection? Do they have a variety of price ranges? Are they orderly or jumbled? Parkas can be bought for very cold zones (with "down" fill), for spring skiing (very light), and for everyday skiing. Ideally, all garments should be versatile enough to be worn for other sports during other seasons as well.

If a garment is expensive and you want to get your money's worth, look for:

- Style – reversibility of some items.
- Design – the kind that will last for several years.
- Good quality fabrics. Designer is a *skier* who knows what the breed wants: economical warmth, careful workmanship throughout, even in case of unseen details.
- Stitching – solid.
- Quality zippers (you can test a zipper by sliding it up and down).

Some people resist the yearly changing fashion parade. The latest ski fashions are less important at the non-"in" places or the small North American ski areas. You'll be at ease in last year's plain sweater (which can be worn for summer hikes, too) or the somewhat short two-year-old parka. *If you don't have to shop for the latest ski wear, your vacation costs less.* Budget-conscious? The *regular* apparel sections of Penney's, Sears, or Montgomery Ward (and other such stores) sell excellent water-repellent parkas often made of the same fabrics as name brands. Army surplus stores may also be worth visiting. Teenagers and even adults now ski in jeans. (One disadvantage, though: jeans can get wet and won't protect you from severe cold.)

You can also buy chic close-fitting stretch pants. The latter are made of textiles that stretch as you ski, fall or sit, then snap back into place. The material won't let through snow. Good stretch pants cost less money. They insulate against the wind. They look elegant. And they'll last many years unless your figure changes. (The skier who is a bit on the heavy side may prefer black.) What's the best fit? Snugness around waist and hips.

If the stretch pants or the ever-more-popular one-piece ski suits are too costly, you might consider warm-up pants that protect your shins, knees, and stomach from chilly winds (and also hide that old pair of slacks). Warm-ups are practical rather than stylish; in fact, they can look sloppy. Unless you plan to ski in spring, dress for cold weather and always be prepared for rapid changes in temperatures.

To protect themselves, both men and women adopt the layer system of cloth-

A warm hat keeps the whole body warm. (SIA)

ing for the slopes. Next to your skin wear an absorbent fabric which will not become clammy and won't transmit moisture. Most longjohns work out fine. The next layer consists of a turtleneck garment, followed by a flannel or wool shirt, and a sweater. After the lifts close down, skiers get out of their heavy footwear and into a pair of aprés-ski boots. (Hiking boots or "Moon boots" are possibilities, too.)

Buy a pair of sunglasses for the high country or sunny slopes, or you risk snow blindness in spring. The glasses should be shatterproof. You can ski in blizzard conditions if you own a pair of yellow goggles. Some even have polaroid lenses which adjust to all lighting conditions. Look for good ventilation against fogging. The higher the price, the better the product.

One professional ski instructor adds a few more pointers:

- Don't forget a cap; the head helps heat your entire body.
- Suntan cream is recommended. Buy it in small tubes so you can carry it in your parka or pants' pockets. Some creams or lotions contain a screen which protects you from the sun.
- Don't forget your mittens or gloves; wear them even if the weather is warm.
- Small packages of Kleenex are available at ski shops. A good investment.
- Ski socks don't need to be extra heavy. In fact, you'll be warmer with two

pair of medium-weight socks instead of one heavy pair. Socks are always worn *inside* your stretch pants.
- Boot trees are convenient for both storage and carrying boots but they're not a must. Skip them if you're short of cash. An airline bag can do as well.

MAINTENANCE

You can beat the high costs of skiing if you take good care of your gear and are capable of making small repairs. Beginners sometimes have the odd notion that a ski's dented, uneven running surface will offer a much-needed brake on the hill. Unfortunately, a pock-marked ski cannot be controlled as well; its ride may turn into a jerky, go-stop, fall-down affair, just as missing edges cause a debacle. A first-timer has enough struggles with the mountain without faulty equipment.

New skis now come from the factory with a colorful plastic coat, usually polyethylene. Rocks can play havoc with the hardest material, causing gashes and holes. Should these be repaired? Definitely. The reason is obvious. A bad scratch on the left ski, for instance, will make the right one go faster. Thus, your leg muscles will strain more to keep the uneven skis under control. Any specialty ski shop will patch your ski bottoms without difficulties, removing minor gouges and also sharpening your edges. This work can be done after the ski season; this way, you start a new winter with flawless equipment.

Many skiers find a plastic undercoating sufficient for a good time on the snow. Others insist that a wax on top is needed, too. Racers and advanced skiers always use it, but instructors often recommend waxing for intermediates and novices also. Turns on skis or a straight schuss become a lot smoother with wax. A shop charges one to two dollars for waxing, so you may prefer to do the job yourself.

What sort of wax do you choose? "The harder the snow, the harder the wax" is one good rule. For most skiers, a layer of paraffin will do for every type of skiing. Waxing won't present any difficulties as long as the skis are dry. Old waxes should be removed with a plastic scraper. For the groove under the skis, a screwdriver or a coin may come in handy. When you apply the wax stick spread the wax in one direction only – either up the ski or down. Old-timers used their palms for this job; a cork will also do. Here, too, a little elbow grease pays off with faster and more effortless skiing later on. After the bottom has been rubbed hard, it should shine like a mirror. This done, skis must be stored for twenty minutes – or a night – in a cold area. Snow can stick to freshly waxed skis, so don't put them on the ground immediately.

The importance of your skis' edges should also be stressed. Look for burrs and rough parts after each ski trip. And keep the edges sharp, especially if you head for icy slopes. If you enjoy that sort of thing, you can save money if you get a 10" mill ski file (stores sell them) and do your own edge sharpen-

Beating the Costs of Equipment

ing. Simple deburring is a great help. For complete sharpening, place the file flat on the bottom of the ski near the end and draw it back to the tip with smooth, even strokes. When sharpening the sides, be careful to keep them straight. Do not let the edges slant in on the sides. To take the burr off, use very fine sandpaper.

When you store your skis, or go on a long trip, wipe the edges with oil to prevent rust. Avoid storage in warm areas or near a furnace. And finally, when traveling, use a ski bag.

THREE

Choosing A Ski Area

HOW THE FIRST-TIMER CAN FIND HAPPINESS

Apart from buying your equipment wisely, you should carefully choose the place for your initial outings and subsequent ski trips.

So where do you go? Before the first yearly winter moisture gathers on the meadows, hills, and peaks of North America, new areas spring up like mushrooms. The land is vast, and there is still space for development, despite the already existing 1200 ski areas. Mountains can be "manufactured" even in flat country. A Pennsylvania ski promoter bought some acres, carted in loads of sand, installed snowmaking machinery, and found himself in business. Several western mountain giants still await their first ski lifts. The area explosion was astonishing – expecially during the sixties and seventies.

Many ski places down South make their own snow. You can often ski at night under artificial lights, a special treat. Some places furnish free benches for the views; some have outdoor tables just like in Switzerland. Each ski area wants to please the customer, who is sometimes wooed with one free lesson for each two paid lessons, with free skiing on Monday, with a mid-week ski ticket at a special price, with "Ladies' Days" (that may include hot spiced wine and many other extras).

There is an infinite variety to the bigger ski resorts. (See Chapters 10 and 11 for specific suggestions.) Although they don't like to admit it, some places are chiefly for expert skiers, or for intermediate skiers, or for beginners, and some are for all three. (It all depends on the percentage of steep versus gentle terrain.) Some areas appeal to aprés-skiers, who seek mostly entertainment and night life. Each ski locale differs when it comes to hotels, inns, lodges, and motels. (Not all ski stations can accommodate you overnight.)

Some ski travelers pick a resort on the basis of suitable accommodations. The average family will probably avoid the posh resort, which consists mostly

Choosing a Ski Area **27**

of pricey condo apartments or high-rise hotels. Some American resorts have elegant hostelries with well-staffed front desks, chandeliers, thick carpets, 24-hour telephones, elevators, room service, chrome showers, tubs fit for Roman nobility and balconies to review the ski parade. A couple with a modest income may elect to ski at Loveland Basin, Colorado, on a weekend, staying in nearby Georgetown at a modest motel. American ski area motels, though generally impersonal, do offer all sorts of conveniences, and you may choose a ski center for its new motor hotels. Ski lodges (see details in next chapter) make a resort attractive for those singles who can pay the tab. As you might guess, accommodations near the lifts always cost the most.

WHY SKI AT THE SMALL AREAS

Many nooks and crannies in the Rockies, Sierrras, Cascades, Canadian Cordilleras, White Mountains, Green Mountains, and Poconos offer dozens of possibilities to get you started. Begin with a modest ski place; ignore the mystique of the famous "name" meccas. The more celebrated and the more jet-setty a resort, the more expensive and unsuitable it will be for average-income families. This is especially so if you're just learning and bringing several children as well. Also, don't forget that you pay a premium for ski lessons at a school run by world-renowned ski directors or at famous ski resorts such as Vail or Stowe, to name two examples.

Lesser-known (or just-opened) ski areas are often your best bet. The super resorts have the highest ski lift prices, with costs of about $50 per couple per day. A couple can get the same ski mileage at a smaller place for about one half these rates. Prices are inevitably lower in the non-prestige or unknown places. The skiing may be only average at these places and the short runs won't interest the super-expert, but a husband and wife with children will enjoy their day.

If you are going on your first skiing vacation, a weekend at a small area will be perfect.

You don't need a big mountain with long "vertical drops," i.e., impressive top-to-bottom measurements.

Here's a Denver example: Instead of heading for far away gigantic Aspen, a Denver beginner will find happiness at Silver Creek, just 78 miles west of the state capitol. The area is not far from the famous Rocky Mountain National Park, with a variety of skiing at a fair price. This comparatively new spot has gained a reputation as a family pleaser, too. (Its vertical will remind you of the U.S. Midwest instead of Colorado.) Even on weekends, the three well-oiled lifts whir in comparative silence. You can transpose this example to any U.S. ski state or Canadian ski province.

If you live in states with limited skiing, you need not travel far away. Content yourself at first with one or two chairlifts. Better skiers might pick *newer*

Beginners don't need super-steep slopes—a small hill will do for the first efforts. (Utah Travel Council)

resorts; the latter show more eagerness to give their customers a financial break. Dozens of little ski hills in Ontario and Wisconsin, and a few in Illinois, attract the less moneyed middle-class skier with kids. Small motels or cabins abound, and ski week rates are affordable if you keep away from the more famous middle western resorts. (Boyne Mountain, Michigan, for example, is expensive.)

Expert skiers are apt to sell the Midwest short because the ski runs *are* short and the elevations low. Yet the Midwest (or its Canadian counterpart) can get ample snow (and features snowmaking machinery besides), so you always *can* enjoy yourself. And dozens of ski places come with sufficient basic uphill machinery – including old-fashioned T-bars or Poma lifts – that provide pleasant exercise for hundreds of new skiers. Much of America's ski history was written in this region. Some of our great ski jumpers and our cross-country skiers hail from these states, where families are devoted to the sport. (For specific suggestions see end of chapter.)

Eastern U.S. skiing is distinguished by excellent satellite facilities such as ski lodges with a tradition and superb restaurants. The accommodation situation in New England is especially appealing. The terrain at Stowe, Vermont, or Mt. Tremblant, Quebec, can satisfy any type of skier.

When you consider weather, quality of snow, and friendliness, the U.S. West has a lot going for it. You tan the easiest at higher elevations. You find fewer people on these vast mountains that reach up to 14,000 feet in the Rockies. You get more space for yourself, more lifts for your convenience, and a look

Choosing a Ski Area

at more advanced skiers whom you can copy. (The Rockies give plenty of competition to the Alps.)

There is plenty of skiing in the Pacific Northwest, on Mt. Hood, Oregon, and under Mt. Rainier, Washington, and further north in British Columbia. Unlike the Alps, which sometimes get snows in little and late doses, the U.S. Northwest and British Columbia see tons of the wonderful stuff descending heavily and early. Only Chile, Australia, and a few isolated spots in Switzerland offer as much solid summer skiing as our American Northwest.

To get down to more details about North American places and accommodations, study the Bibliography at the end of this book. Also read the detailed descriptions of the best known resorts in Chapters 10 and 11.

Here are some of the less familiar U.S. ski areas to get you started.

A LIST FOR NOVICES

State and Ski Area	Location (Nearest Town)
California	
Donner Ski Ranch	Norden
Holiday Hill	Wrightwood
Colorado	
Breckenridge	Breckenridge
Loveland Basin	Georgetown
Silver Creek	Granby
Connecticut	
Ski Sundown	New Hartford
Idaho	
Bogus Basin	Boise
Schweitzer Basin	Sandpoint
Maine	
Squaw Mountain	Greenville
Sugarloaf	Carrabassett Valley
Massachusetts	
Bousquet	Pittsfield
Michigan	
Alpine Valley	Milford
Caberfae	Cadillac
Montana	
Bridger Bowl	Bozeman
Big Mountain	Whitefish
Nevada	
Slide Mountain	Reno
Mt. Rose	Reno

State and Ski Area	Location (Nearest Town)
New Hampshire	
King Ridge	New London
Gunstock	Laconia
New Jersey	
Hidden Valley	Vernon
Vernon Valley Great Gorge	McAfee
New Mexico	
Santa Fe Ski Area	Santa Fe
Sandia Peak	Albuquerque
New York	
Snow Ridge	Turin
Big Vanilla at Davos	Woodridge
Hunter Mountain	Hunter
Oregon	
Mt. Hood Meadows	Mt. Hood
Mt. Bachelor	Bend
Pennsylvania	
Camelback	Tannersville
Seven Springs	Champion
Utah	
Brighton	Brighton
Sundance	Provo
Vermont	
Magic Mountain	Londonderry
Pico Peak	Rutland
Washington	
Mt. Baker	Bellingham
White Pass Village	White Pass
Wisconsin	
Telemark Ski Area	Cable

A Few Resorts in Canada

British Columbia	
Kimberly Ski Resort	Kimberly
Red Mountain	Rossland
Ontario	
Calabogie Peaks	Calabogie
Candy Mountain	Thunder Bay

Choosing a Ski Area

Quebec
  Mont-Sutton
  Mont Sainte-Anne
  Sutton
  Beaupré

SKI AREA CHECKLIST

Here are some final questions to help you determine your particular situation:

- Does the area have a rental shop? Are there sufficient pairs of skis and boots for a busy weekend?
- Is there a nursery willing to accept children of all age groups, including your tots?

Some ski resorts specialize in children's instruction. (Winter Park, CO)

Large resorts such as Stratton, Vermont, have a lot of packing equipment, which assures you smooth slopes. (Schriebl)

Choosing a Ski Area 33

- Does the ski place have a reputation for beginners and recreational skiers or mostly for downhill and slalom racing?
- Are there special lift ticket rates for older people? Free skiing for seniors?
- What's the cutoff age for children's lift tickets?
- Are there cross-country trails? If so, are the X-C trails maintained? Are they free or is there a fee?
- Will there be crowd scenes on weekends?
- Are there accommodations in the vicinity or only at the bottom of the hill at premium rates?
- Is there an emphasis on intermediate terrain, with good slope grooming? Will average skiers be coddled here or is the management only interested in hotshots, hotdoggers (ski acrobats) and professional ski speed events?
- Is there enough snow? Does the area have snowmaking?
- Are the access roads from your home to the resort, and around it, usually passable, or will there be bumper-to-bumper traffic problems on weekends?
- Will a non-skiing family member be happy here? Will there be enough activities for him or her?
- And one of the most important questions: Has the ski center maintained a friendly, cheery, helpful attitude or become an impersonal overstaffed complex where more skiers are not welcome?

FOR MORE INFORMATION ON U.S. SKI AREAS, WRITE TO:

Alaska Division of Tourism
Department of Commerce and Economic Development
Pouch E, State Capitol
Juneau, Alaska 99811

California State Office of Tourism
1400 Tenth Street
Sacramento, California 95814

Colorado Division of Commerce and Development
602 State Capitol Annex
Denver, Colorado 80203

Connecticut Department of Commerce
210 Washington St.
Hartford, Connecticut 06106

Delaware Travel Development Bureau
Division of Economic Development
630 College Road
Dover, Delaware 19901

Idaho Division of Tourism and Industrial Development
Room 108
Statehouse
Boise, Idaho 83720

Illinois Division of Tourism
222 South College Street
Springfield, Illinois 62706

Maine Department of Commerce and Industry
Augusta, Maine 04330

Maryland Tourist Development
1748 Forest Drive
Annapolis, Maryland 21401

Massachusetts Division of Tourism
100 Cambridge Street
Boston, Massachusetts 02202

Michigan Tourist Council
300 South Capitol Avenue
Suite 102
Lansing, Michigan 48926

Minnesota Department of Economic Development
Vacation Information Center
Hanover Building
480 Cedar
St. Paul, Minnesota 55101

Montana Chamber of Commerce
P.O. Box 1730
Helena, Montana 59601

Nebraska Department of Economic Development
301 Centennial Mall South
P.O. Box 94666
State Capitol
Lincoln, Nebraska 68509

Nevada Travel Tourism Division
Carson City, Nevada 89701

New Hampshire Division of Parks and Recreation
P.O. Box 856
State House Annex
Concord, New Hampshire 03301

New Jersey State Promotion
P.O. Box 400
Trenton, New Jersey 08625

Choosing a Ski Area

New Mexico Department of Development
Tourist Division
113 Washington Ave.
Santa Fe, New Mexico 87803

New York State Department of Commerce
99 Washington Avenue
Albany, New York 12210

North Carolina Travel and Promotion Division
P.O. Box 27687
Raleigh, North Carolina 27602

North Dakota Travel Department
Capitol Grounds
Bismarck, North Dakota 58501

Oregon Travel Information Section
State Transportation Building
Salem, Oregon 97310

Pennsylvania Bureau of Travel Development
431 South Office Building
Harrisburg, Pennsylvania 17120

Utah Travel Council
Council Hall
Salt Lake City, Utah 84114

Vermont Information/Travel Division
61 Elm Street
Montpelier, Vermont 05602

Virginia State Travel Service
6 North 6th St.
Richmond, Virginia 23219

Washington Travel Development Division
101 General Administration Building
Olympia, Washington 98501

West Virginia Travel Development Division
1900 Washington Street, East
Charleston, West Virginia 25305

Wisconsin Division of Tourism
P.O. Box 177
Madison, Wisconsin 53701

Wisconsin Bureau of Vacation and Travel Services
P.O. Box 450
Madison, Wisconsin 53701

Wyoming Travel Commission
2320 Capitol Avenue
Cheyenne, Wyoming 82001

Canada

Tourism Canada
235 Queen Street
Fourth Floor East
Ottawa, Ontario K1A OH6

FOUR

Getting To (And Living Well At) Your Ski Destination

Ski travel, whether for a weekend or a week, takes some planning. Reserve the time to compare the myriad ski offers. Read the newspaper ads, brochures, and magazine articles with care. Investigate, analyze, and compare. Avail yourself of ski travel guides. Unfortunately, many skiers just take off without real preparation. They may spend three times as much money as they should on their ski holiday.

One of the most important parts of preparation is transportation. The right transportation makes a difference.

AUTOMOBILE TRAVEL

In many instances, auto travel is cheaper than air travel for a brief trip and short distances, especially for those who have time and stamina. An Albany, New York, family bound for a few days in Stowe, Vermont, will do better to use their own station wagon than to fly. Likewise, many west Texans flock cheaply to the New Mexico ski resorts by car, and a look at any Colorado ski area parking lot will prove that Nebraskans make up a goodly percentage of Colorado's ski trade.

A car allows you to be more flexible and encourages you to ski at several areas or to change unsuitable accommodations. If you are short on time and fly, use a car rental. First investigate the local rental situation and check the special deals of the big car rental firms. They may have some weekend and weekly rates. But when you arrive at an airport – say, Portland, Washington – also look up the phone numbers of *small* auto rental outfits. You'll find them in the yellow pages of the phone book. Compare rates! Within minutes, you can sit in a compact car. Make sure that it comes with snow tires and a ski rack (no extra charge). In recent years, *older* used vehicles have also become available in some communities at about a third of the cost of the large, overpriced Hertz or Avis offerings. (One such outfit is Rent-A-Wreck.)

Taking your own automobile requires some research and some prior map study. You must figure out your possible mileage and time factors in advance. You might consider taking extra passengers and sharing expenses. And if you are to travel in high mountain country, be familiar with the hazards of driving in snow.

WINTER DRIVING

Thanks to 24,833 miles of mountain roads, and an October-to-May ski season, Coloradans have learned a few tricks about winter driving. But no matter where you live – in New England, in the Midwest, the California Sierras, the Pacific Northwest – you may have to cope with snow and ice. Here are some pointers.

To start with, make sure that your car is ready before you venture into a blizzard. Have it checked by a mechanic. Is the motor tuned up? Do the brakes function well? Do you have a good battery? Are your headlights and tail lights okay? When visibility is poor, cars often plow into one another because tail lights don't work. Does your trunk contain a shovel and a bag of sand (in case you get stuck) and tire chains for deep-snow conditions? Do you carry extra gas and is your tank full? (One more tip: A warm blanket and some extra food reserves might come in handy.)

On packed snow or ice, of course, your tires are of critical importance. Slick tires are like sleds: You can't stop them. Radials are helpful, but better still, invest in a pair of cleated snow tires; the thick knobs bite into fresh snow. "Studs" are permissible in most eastern and western states during the winter. (Studs will give you a sure traction even in the worst conditions.)

Under blizzard conditions, especially if you have rear wheel drive or an automatic one, nothing can match chains. Proof? The National Safety Council and the American Automobile Club ran an interesting experiment. They let a sub-compact slide at 20 m.p.h. across a patch of ice. On regular tires, it took the car 180 feet to stop! They then equipped the same Ford's rear wheels with tire chains. The car now braked within 70 feet! So it's understandable why certain mountain highways (up to the Continental Divide in Colorado, or Donner Pass in California, or Mt. Hood, Oregon) are sometimes barred to vehicles *without* chains.

Mounting tire chains isn't every skier's dish of sherbert. Just ask a service station to do the job. They will. While you're in a station, take a look at the thermometer. If the roads have been wet, and the temperature is 32 or lower, you may face ice conditions. (Warm ice can be just as bad or worse, by the

Getting to (and Living Well at) Your Ski Destination **39**

way.) How do you handle it? Use restraint and steadiness. Skidding can be a bone-chilling experience. Advice: Steer the car in the direction of the skid. In other words, if the vehicle is skidding to the left, the front wheels should be turned to the left until the vehicle begins to straighten out.

Some more hints:

- Starting slowly provides better traction and prevents spinning the wheels or skidding sideways into parked cars or other vehicles or objects. When starting on a slick surface, use the second gear to keep the car's wheels from spinning. Stopping slowly can prevent skidding. If the vehicle starts to skid or the wheels lock on a slick road, release the brake pressure. Instead, pump or tap the brakes lightly under these conditions.
- Be on the lookout for hidden or shaded ice spots that remain on curves after the road has been cleared.
- Whenever visibility becomes so poor, due to fog or snow, that you can't see more than a few feet ahead, pull off the road and clean your windshield or wait until the weather eases up.
- If you *must* drive in fog or a snowstorm, always use the lower headlight beam. The upper one will glance off the fog and irritate your eyes.
- Don't be afraid of mountain driving. Most winter accidents actually happen on straight, open, level highways.

One final consideration: The type of vehicle you buy has much to do with how you'll handle difficult conditions. *Skiers should generally stick to front wheel drive vehicles.* Most U.S. auto makers now manufacture such models, or you might consider the renowned Swedish imports (Saab, Volvo), German cars (Volkswagen), or some of the better Japanese front wheel models (Honda, Subaru, and others).

GOING BY SKI TRAIN

Many winter travelers never bother to look into the availability of a special ski train to take them to their favorite area. Amtrak's services and the Canadian railroads have been improved. A rail trip is of special interest to families with children who will welcome the unique experience.

Some ski trains cover short distances and are therefore ideal for one day of skiing. Other rails work out well for the weekend or for a full week's skiing. North America's notable ski trains include the following:

- The Denver-Winter Park, Colorado, skier's special takes off every Saturday morning with a cargo of 800 youngsters and a sprinkling of adults.
- From Portland, Oregon, you can travel by rail to Boise, from where you head to Sun Valley, Idaho. Inquire at your Amtrak office.
- An overnighter from Chicago travels to New Mexico, serving areas like Taos Ski Valley.

Ski trains should always be considered for transportation, if available. (Kris Rud)

- The Laurentians, just north of Montreal, can be reached every day via Amtrak's Montrealer. This well-known train makes several stops in Vermont on its daily run from cities like Washington D.C., Baltimore, New York, and Philadelphia. On another train to Montreal, the Adirondack, connections can be arranged at Rhinecliff for the Catskills, and at Hudson for the Berkshires, and at Albany-Rensselaer for the Adirondacks.
- Originating in Chicago, the California Zephyr departs for Denver, Salt Lake City, and San Francisco all year long, with a popular stop in Granby, Colorado. Skiers then transfer to express buses that take them to several areas. The Zephyr also stops in Glenwood Springs to let off Aspen-bound skiers.
- Amtrak's famous longtime "Empire Builder" serves several ski areas in Montana, including Big Mountain (from Minneapolis/St. Paul and Seattle/Portland).
- From San Francisco a railway heads to Schweitzer Basin, Idaho, or Snowbird and Alta, Utah, via Ogden, Utah.
- The Coast Starlight/Daylight makes a daily 1361-mile run between Los Angeles and Seattle, with connecting trains to San Diego and Vancouver. Destinations: Sierras, Cascades, Cordilleras.
- Californians can also take the Mt. Bachelor Ski Train from Sacramento, Oakland, and other cities every Saturday and Sunday.
- The "Olympian Skier's Special" connects New York's Grand Central Station with the Lake Placid region.

EUROPEAN TRAINS

If you're skiing in Europe, keep in mind that German, Austrian, and Swiss railways are outstanding. For prolonged skiing in the Alps, Pyrenees, and Scandinavia, your best bet is to order a *Eurailpass*. (You get it in the U.S.)

As a Eurailpass customer, you pay a lump sum for a set period (two weeks, for example), which entitles you to unlimited travel on some 100,000 miles of rails. You travel in first-class compartments, with plenty of upholstery, a tiny table for your brown bag lunch, beverage service via a cart, or a dining car. The trains run quietly day and night.

Nearly 1,800 locomotives ply the rails of just one little Alpine nation, Switzerland. Most of the system is electric, smokeless and noiseless. The Swiss have always made sure that their rolling stock and services are of the highest quality. The railroads run on schedule like the best watches. The Austrian trains to places like St. Anton and Innsbruck are punctual, too. The German *Eisenbahnen* live up to your expectations: never a delay; access to the far corners like Garmisch, Bavaria; clean carriages with white linen. On the trains, you get to know Europeans, many of whom speak English. Unless you travel at peak periods, you should have no seating problems. Some people prefer to make reservations for some of the super trains (like France's *Aquitaine*, Italy's *Settebello* and others.) The Eurail network includes 16 countries. Variety!

For instance, the longest Finnish rail route (ideal for cross-country skiing) takes you beyond the Arctic Circle and into the clean landscape of Lapland. Sweden's crack electrified trains run to the Midnight Sun region. Fast through trains operate between Stockholm and Gothenburg on the sunny west coast of Sweden or between Stockholm and Malmo in the south.

If you want to restrict yourself to one country, inquire ahead of time about a special ticket. The Swiss, for example, sell an eight-day Holiday Pass for skiers, as well as a Senior Citizen's Pass.

Always inquire about dining cars ahead of time. If the train has none, you can stop for picnic supplies at Europe's major stations. Munich's and Zurich's are typical with their many stores.

A few francs, marks or schillings pay for shipping your luggage in the special baggage car. Don't rely on your suitcase's prompt arrival, particularly if you change trains frequently. It took this writer two days to receive a suitcase in St. Anton from Garmisch.

USING BUSES

Special U.S. ski buses are now common. Such buses originate in many major cities, with each vehicle bound for a ski resort. There are short and long bus trips, daily ones, and some catering to the weekend customers. There are express buses that pick up skiers at airports. Your local bus station can provide details. For example, Killington, one of Vermont's major resorts, is accessible via regularly scheduled bus service from Philadelphia, New Jersey, New York, Washington, and Baltimore. A number of bus companies also offer complete vacation packages. One weekend express departs Thursday to Killington and returns Sunday. Another express leaves for Vermont on Sunday morning and gets you home again Friday night. Many ski tour operators can be contacted at 800 numbers.

AIR CARRIERS

Long-distance driving is slow business, especially at 55 miles an hour. Flying to a far-away resort therefore fills the ski traveler's need, particularily for one or two persons. Because of competition for the skier's dollar, airlines choose the most direct routes and best schedules, especially on weekends.

Airlines provide free (and generally accurate) snow reports. Some airlines can make reservations at ski lodges for you and teletype in advance for rental cars. Before departure time, an airport porter takes your skis and poles. He slides them into a long cardboard box or a see-through plastic bag. (There is no charge for the box, and skis go as part of your baggage.) The block-long jet awaits, ready to whisk you to your destination.

Some chartered ski flights offer spiced wine or even champagne as a bonus, all part of your package. On some planes, you'll find ski publications or in-flight magazines with special ski articles, and the personnel, even the captain, may be skiers. In just a few hours, you land in Vermont or New Mexico or Austria.

When planning, inquire about special family plans, group fares, and round-trip rates. Your travel agent will know *which* airline has the best deals at the moment by checking the computers. The best travel agents are members of *Asta*, a trade association. And some agents are CTC's, i.e., they've passed an exam to be a Certified Travel Counselor.

A competent travel agent is more than a ticket vendor but a specialist whose experience and know-how enables him or her to advise you on every aspect of your winter vacation. America's 22,500 or so travel agents are appointed by transportation companies to issue tickets and officially represent the carriers. Naturally, not every agency knows the ski business. The ones that do can save you a lot of time.

Ski vacationers often harbor the misconception that these agencies charge you more for tickets than the airlines. Not so. You merely pay something extra when you ask for a complex itinerary that requires many long distance calls. You'll have to reimburse some of those expenses. And be aware that certain hotel rooms may cost more if an agent books them for you.

SKI PACKAGES

There isn't much work involved in laying the groundwork for your ski weekend at a nearby hill or quick short flight to the nearest resort. A full ski vacation entails more, however, particularly if you want to stay at a first-class ski lodge, pre-arrange lessons, and do it all at the lowest possible cost with one check.

A simple solution is a pre-packaged ski vacation, also known as the Ski Week. (Some packages are for only five days or less, however.) Ski resort associations, resort-based tor operators, sell all-inclusive packages with or without transportation. Or you may prefer the travel agent package, which includes in some cases your (sometimes lower) airfare, airport-to-resort transfers as well as lodging, and daily shuttle to the slope, lift tickets, and some complimentary surprises.

A ski deal is practical for travelers who are pressed for time. The package contains most of the components for your vacation. The price may range from $300 to $800 a week, depending on accommodations and extras, plus flight. A ski package caters to your convenience, eliminating a lot of correspondence. A single call does it all. Besides, a Ski Week costs less than if you were to buy each item separately.

Some ski resorts work with airlines who offer special fares if you buy the resort package. One example is the compact, well-run Keystone ski resort in Colorado. For many seasons now, Keystone's management has arranged for cheaper airline tickets to Denver from some 80 cities, as long as you buy a ski tour package. The latter allows you to stay at Keystone's sleek Ski Lodge for five nights (kids under 12 stay free), with four days of skiing, plus gratis transportation from the airport, which is 75 miles away.

By calling your favorite resort – east or west, north or south – you'll no doubt uncover similar deals. The Killington ski area in Vermont, for example, has long marketed special early or late season packages with all kinds of possibilities. (You can even opt for three or four days instead of a week.)

Likewise, the airlines sometimes promote deals that include more than just the flight, often in concert with tour operators. Here's a typical "Skifari" package offered by one airline to Calgary, Alberta, and the famous Banff resort:

- Special round-trip economy air fare.
- Seven days–six nights hotel/motel accommodations, based on double occupancy.
- Transportation from Calgary airport to Banff and return motor coach.
- Five round-trip transfers between hotel/motel pick-up points and Sunshine, Mount Norquay, or Lake Louise ski areas.
- Ski lift tickets for five days valid in Sunshine, Mount Norquay, and Lake Louise.

- Special rates at the hotel in downtown Calgary for those who may wish to spend an extra night or more in Calgary prior to or after the week in Banff.

From certain cities you can also buy a ski holiday at reduced airfares. The principle here is the group fare at a solid discount. (Your airline sometimes forms the group.) Such deals often force you to buy land arrangements.

Budget-minded skiers may also take advantage of the airline's bargain "supersaver" fares which may offer discounts of about 30-50 percent off regular coach fares for travel Tuesday through Thursday. Seats are limited and must be booked a few weeks in advance. The occasional price wars among the airlines make this a *passenger's* market! Discounts on ground packages which include lodging, car rental, and ski lessons may also be available through the airlines. You can book such a tour at major airline counters or through your travel agent.

The best winter packages are available to people who belong to an organization that can get charter air fares. Members of ski clubs in Texas, Florida (yes, even Florida has ski clubs), and Illinois, for example, live it up at a low cost in some of the nation's finest resorts. Charter flights are available to skiers who travel as members of a large group, who select their specific destination, departure and return dates, and aircraft type. Trips are usually booked *six* months in advance. On some charter flights, you get first-class amenities, including gratis liquor, free ski bags, and snow and weather condition reports.

What are the requirements for a group that needs an entire plan? Here are the official rules that apply to one typical charter:

- The group, club, or organization must be organized for purposes other than travel (i.e., travel clubs are not eligible).
- Members wishing to travel with the group must have belonged to the organization for a minimum of six months.
- Only a member and his or her dependent household members are eligible, unless opened to the public, which requires special financial provisions such as consumer protection bonds.

Other possibilities for ski travel include the U.S. Ski Association which occasionally gets into the travel business, and AAA travel departments. Even Amtrak sells packages. Consider also joining an Air Travel Club. Specialized air travel clubs can offer more reasonable rates than commercial carriers because these clubs have fewer overhead expenses. Unlike the regular airlines, air travel clubs shell out little or no money for advertising. To become eligible for their cut-rate flights, you first pay an initiation fee and then annual membership dues. In addition, some clubs exact a yearly contribution for the operation of their aircrafts.

Ski vacation packages are normally put together by travel experts who know the ski business and skiers' needs. You often profit from the expertise of a per-

Getting to (and Living Well) at Your Ski Destination   **45**

son who lives near the ski center of your choice. Irrespective of who sells it, a ski package generally means reduced lift rates. After all, ticket costs are based on the length of your stay at a resort, and lift rates always go down if you ski for several days. (At one typical big-time resort, Sun Valley, Idaho, the five-day lift ticket is much cheaper than the very expensive daily rate.)

Many of the ski weeks are put together by resort associations, but you can also look into deals from a motel group, several combined ski areas, or a promotion-minded ski lodge. Study the details before laying out your hard-earned money. Some travelers may be swayed by bonuses that are not always desirable. If you were to buy five nights at a Nevada resort, for instance, your package may include $5 worth of free casino chips per adult, four complimentary cocktails, and a free Casino fondue party.

Yet some offers yield excellent value, with the bonuses adding up. A look into the brochure of the well-run, well-advertised, and always well-occupied Beaver's Village Ski Lodge (Winter Park, Colorado) shows some ideal ski week components. Among these:

- Individual room accommodations for seven nights.
- Breakfast and dinner with all-you-can-eat soup and salad.
- Unlimited use of 14 lifts for seven days.
- Ski movies.
- Genuine ski lodge atmosphere.
- Free sauna and Jacuzzi whirlpools, game room, ping pong.
- Free coffee all day long.
- Moonlight cross-country tours at a nearby touring center.
- Lodge location at major bus stop.
- Free shuttle service to and from ski area all day. (The latter can make a difference to those without a car.)

When shopping for value, you might scan brochures for important clues: How many nights do you get for your lump sum? How many meals? Does the package offer airport-to-ski area transportation? A rental car? Will you get free ski lessons? Does the resort feature children's programs? Will your family get in enough skiing? Will you have to share a room? (Some packages stipulate "four per room.") Does the resort have a reputation for overcrowding? Will you be penalized for traveling alone?

Try to read between the lines. A ski area may advertise "from $399" a week but in reality the week will cost you $500. Unfortunately, one area may only give you five motel nights and five lift passes; you buy your own meals and everything else.

The five-day idea (and in some cases only three days) never works out as well as the seven-day package. To be sure, the longer you stay the more you save. Some resorts actually give you one free day with six. Incidentally, the packages are cheapest *before* Thanksgiving or before December 10, during the first week of January and in April. You should always examine the descriptions of the actual hostelries in your ski package. "The Yodler" may well turn out to be a dormitory for collegians, and the "As low as $199 a Week!!!" could mean an inferior hotel, with your bath down the hall. The transfer from plane to area may be at your own expense, and there could be a clause that if you must cancel, only part of your deposit will be returned. (Resort hotels sometimes keep your entire deposit if you cancel a peak season reservation.)

Ask yourself as you study an offering: Do I really need ski lessons? Will my companion want to take lessons? Will I actually use up seven days worth of lift tickets? If you like to alternate between downhill and cross-country, the package should allow you to do so.

An expert skier should find out if the ski school has a good reputation and employs top instructors (see Chapter 7). Older skiers may not be interested in "free fondue parties" for which they may have to pay as a part of the ski package. Lastly, when dealing with a resort association, make sure to call their free 800 number if they have one.

EUROPEAN PACKAGES

Ski Weeks are sold to and in Alpine countries, too. The idea has worked out so well that international carriers like Air Canada whisk tour customers not only to the Canadian Rockies but also to the Alps. Swissair holds out such skier's gems as St. Moritz, Klosters, Davos, and St. Anton (from New York, Chicago, Montreal). Ski-tripping overseas is cheapest from early January through Feburary. A variety of economical and flexible ski packages are always available for January, too. Such Alpine packages can be booked for one, two and three weeks at a combination of different European resorts with two or three meals a day, service, tax, ski instruction and use of all lifts.

A popular annual pre-season ski package is marketed by the Swiss airline, Swissair (see appendix for addresses). One lump sum includes everything except transportation, at such choice resorts as Andermatt (a true Alpine gem), Grindelwald, Arosa, and others. Why the deal? 1) Instructors come to these areas for their refresher courses and for the renewal of their licenses, and students are welcome. 2) Few ski tourists think of heading for resorts before Christmas, yet the beds are available. Thousands of skiers from all over the world take advantage of these Swiss bargain weeks.

If you arrive with your own group of a dozen people or more, you can also get a ski deal from certain Swiss hotels which own their own ski buses and transport you to various nearby ski resorts. Typically such packages are offered by several hotels in Zurich. Likewise, several Munich, West Germany, hotels arrange some group trips to Garmisch and other German ski locales. These deals allow you to choose your own air carrier at the lowest possible price.

ARRANGING YOUR OWN U.S. ACCOMMODATIONS

You can also write to the resort itself before your arrival and ask to see brochures and descriptions of places to stay (with rates). For singles or well-heeled couples and families, America's ski lodges are ideal, but the better rooms may cost more than you want to pay. A thorough study of the situation usually results in some valuable finds.

To illustrate: A reasonable "Ski and Stay Package" is offered for five slope-side days and nights at the Bolton Valley Resort in Vermont. Included are accommodations at the Bolton Valley Lodge, unlimited use of lifts, cross-country fees, the use of the sports club, plus daily exercise classes. One affordable rate covers double occupancy for the five-day, five-night plan; a few extra dollars buys lessons and even a video diagnosis of your skiing. One advantage to these packages is that you know everything in advance.

The American Plan (with all meals) and Modified American Plan (without lunch) aren't as popular as they used to be a decade ago. But when you find them, these plans *can* mean some savings. At certain ski lodges in the West,

One possibility is a studio apartment. It usually offers cooking facilities. (Canadian Government Tourist Office)

for example, M.A.P. packages do not cost much more than European Plan (without meals) at several resorts. On the other hand, these arrangements obligate you to dine at your lodge or hotel, even if the meals turn out to be poor. If you prefer to try a different restaurant every night, which is always possible at bigger resorts, this plan is not ideal.

Alternatives are numerous. A couple can often find a simple motel with cooking facilities. You can stay in a guest house or in a private home at a reasonable price. Bed and breakfast deals exist, too. Dormitories satisfy many young people. It is sometimes possible to rent a cabin. Certainly condos are practical for a group of four or more people. To save on food costs, make breakfast your big meal, with plenty of ham and eggs, toast and jam. You can bring your own sandwich for lunch; few areas have objections to "brown-baggers." A mountain top picnic in the sun can be especially enjoyable.

Most modern ski resorts offer small and large condominiums, too. (Sugarbush Valley, VT)

A more modest condo like this complex offers low prices for large groups who share the units. This particular complex is popular with ski clubs. (Hi Country Haus, Winter Park, CO)

Wherever you go, keep in mind that the week between Christmas and New Year's plus Easter vacations are the most hectic times for ski resorts. In general, western ski areas are full during the month of March. So you'll definitely need an early reservation (send a deposit). Ski resorts near large cities can be jammed on weekends; it is therefore best to make arrangements beforehand. Remember that mail is sometimes slow; to save time and get a quick confirmation, it often pays to call long distance – especially to an 800 number.

So much for peak periods. During the remainder of the ski season, unless it's college vacation time or there is a big race, you may be able to get a bed without confirming one beforehand.

HOW TO PACK FOR A SKI VACATION

Experienced winter vacationers usually travel light, especially by air. Minimum weight becomes crucial if you want to ski in Europe. You're allowed only 62 pounds on a flight. Resorts all over the world have become more informal; many skiers therefore plan to wear ski clothes almost exclusively. For dinner or a casual evening in the lodge lounge, they merely change to slightly dressier and lighter-weight sweaters, along with slacks and after-ski boots. A down-filled parka is light yet warm enough. Some parkas do double duty as city wear.

Women skiers should aim for "double-duty clothes," like versatile ski suits, or slacks that can be worn on and off the slopes. Build around basic colors. Fashion cooperates with clothes in no-iron jerseys, wrinkle-resistant synthetics, wash and wear blends and knits. Three sets of lingerie – one to wear, one to wash, one spare – is plenty for any trip. Spillables, like tubes of hair spray, shaving cream, suntan lotion, and hair tonics, belong in plastic lined cases. Bring a spot remover you've tested at home, instant towelettes, and laundry soap capsules. For long trips miniature drying lines can be handy.

How does the ski traveler pack? Suitcase packing is never totally wrinkle free. But after years of testing, at least one luggage factory has devised a system that comes close. It is designed for efficient use of space, quick location of what you want out of the bag, fast fabric recovery, and accessibility. A divider results in two suitcases in one. Put shoes, accessories, underclothes, and sportswear on one side, dresses and suits on the other. Pack in sections, for instance, underwear together, sportswear together. Removal of clothes and re-packing is quicker by this method and means fewer creases than putting layers of different size garments on top of each other.

Cushion each fabric fold with the fold of another fabric instead of tissue paper. Fold crushable materials over cushioning layers of uncrushables such as knitted sweaters. Heavy items go at the bottom of the case, resting on the hinges at the back. Place shoes, alarm clocks, electric shavers, etc., near the hinges to avoid shifting and wrinkling clothes in transit. Distribute the weight evenly from side to side. For instance, place two pairs of shoes opposite each other, each pair heel-to-toe. (Socks fit neatly into shoes, too.) A balanced suitcase is easier to carry. Fold practically everything (slacks excepted) lengthwise, in three sections, following body curves. This will minimize wrinkles.

And finally, if your luggage is misplaced, don't panic. Report it immediately to the air carrier and be patient. Bus lines, for example, will often ask you to wait a day before filing for a loss. Lost luggage usually turns up.

FIVE

All About Skiing Inexpensively

ECONOMY SKIING FOR AVERAGE PEOPLE

Economy skiing anyone? It *can* be done. Just heed the ground rules laid down by America's "ski bums," the men and women who are serious about the sport and can never get enough of it. Ski bums ski the most for the least money. Even a professional person will learn something from the clan.

The savings campaign begins at home. The young crowd shuns the fancy ski magazine advertisements for fashions, and you will seldom see our youth looking at the ski finery in elegant department stores. Think in the same vein; concentrate on your ski holiday and throw out fashion consciousness. Instead, use the money for travel. As long as you have well-fitted ski boots, suitable (not fashionable) skis, and reliable bindings, you're in business. Instead of buying after-ski or moon boots, use your hiking or climbing boots. You will be best off by paying for equipment and your accommodations in cash. Charge accounts or credit cards increase your expenses by as much as 18 percent unless you pay in 30 days (few shoppers do).

The second savings possibility is in your transportation to the ski action. Again, thousands of young enthusiasts wouldn't be on the slopes unless they took all sorts of shortcuts. One shortcut is to *pool* car rides to the areas. This is an especially sensible measure in view of energy conservation and the ever-increasing gas prices and auto repair expenses. Assemble a few other passengers for a 100-mile ride to your favorite area, and – lo! – you pay less for the trip. (You share the cost, of course.) Ski areas, associations, and shops often arrange for automobile passengers or even run bus trips at special rates. You can also check bulletin boards. Young people even resort to a cheaper route: hitchhike to the area.

THE ADVANTAGE OF SKI CLUBS

Average wage earners of various ages should also consider the possibility of joining a ski club for cut-rate transportation and lodging. Ski or recreational clubs practically guarantee economy skiing. Ditto for the large professional organizations. Many clubs charter buses through the winter. Or they organize car pools. Clubs also arrange for joint discounts on trains and planes. A Texas club regularly moves its members to Aspen for a long weekend, and one club in Boston even arranged a flight to ski in Australia. The Flatland Ski Association, which encompasses ski clubs in Kansas, Oklahoma, Missouri, Iowa, and Nebraska, brings as many as 1500 skiers to a resort; this gives the club some clout for discounts and special favors. Vermont's Killington, for instance, allows a discount on lifts, lessons, equipment, and lodging to groups of only 20 people; for every 20 more, there is even a complimentary lift pass.

The sales director of a western area put it this way: "Some groups travel here as a busload. We have dozens of church groups which arrive on buses from Oklahoma and Texas each winter, because many of the churches own buses, and it's a reasonable drive from these states. Our atmosphere is wholesome and safe for the families and kids. They know they can have a good time here without worrying about big city or "fast-lane resort" influences. We even provide space for devotionals, an excellent inexpensive meal plan, and various activities for our teenagers to enjoy in the evening."

Some ski clubs own their own chalets in the mountains, where you can stay for practically nothing. In addition, certain clubs often have senior members who teach you to ski for the fun of it. They're not certified instructors but just advanced skiers; they get a kick out of doing their share.

Clubs vary, in image, groups, emphasis, and activities. If you lived in Denver, for example, there is the Eskimo Ski Club, which concentrates strictly on youngsters aged from nine to seventeen. Every Saturday, more than a thousand Eskimos board a special ski train for ski lessons in the Colorado Rockies. This is but one of 60 ski clubs in Denver. Most larger cities near the ski belts have a similar variety. If you join, you are expected to do your part. To get the name of the nearest organization, you can write to the U.S. Ski Association (see appendix for address) or contact one of the divisional association offices in the country.

A final tip: Does your professional organization-association ever hold a convention at a major ski resort? If so, you profit doubly – first, via special rates, second through a hefty income tax writeoff.

SPECIAL LIFT RATES

You can reduce the cost of skiing in other ways. Lift tickets, for example, are cheaper by the season if you are on the slopes more than 25 times. Many areas offer family rates. A few places will even let a youngster under 12 go

All About Skiing Inexpensively 53

free if the skier brings a parent along. If you plan to ski for three or more days, you are best off with multiple tickets for the whole period; buying your pass by the day would be far more expensive. In addition, there are student rates, and, conversely, many resorts let seniors ski for free. (You need to be over 65, and in a few cases over 70.)

It is possible to earn a half-day ticket by helping to bus dishes at the ski area cafeteria and by doing other chores. Ski bums are known for finding temporary part-time area jobs to earn lift tickets.

Beginners will save by choosing those rare ski areas that still feature primitive lifts like T-Bars or Pomas instead of tramways and triple chairs. Some places also have bargain rates for chair lifts only; such areas boast a tram or gondola where you pay a premium price for the day's skiing. You might also consider a hike or a little boutique browsing before lunch, and then buy half-day lift tickets. The savings can be as much as 30 percent, and you will still have enough time on the hill.

You should always try to avoid weekend skiing. Ski tickets are wasted when you stand in line with hundreds of other people. Weekends are the vacationers' time to explore Salt Lake City or Boston or other cities in the vicinity of your chosen resort. Day trips are cheapest, of course. You are home again at night and thus don't need to shell out money for the ski resort inn.

In recent years, new developments have taken place to give economy-minded skiers a break. Some larger resorts, for instance, allow local people to buy a special pass which entitles them to a discount. In some parts of the country, especially in the large cities, supermarket chains and sporting goods stores have jumped on the bandwagon. In order to get you to shop at their stores, these big-time retailers sell lift tickets for a nearby ski resort at two to three dollars off. (Watch for ads in your local newspapers.) In addition to this, watch for early or late season deals. And don't forget the wonder of wonders – the single ticket ride – which is perfect for beginning or less ambitious skiers.

Still more suggestions:

- Keep your eyes on new or emerging ski areas in your region, or opt for a newly opened ski spot for your vacation. For promotional purposes, accommodations come with free lift tickets.
- Some resorts generate interest in ski lessons by combining instruction costs with lift access at one advantageous rate.
- Rates are often cheaper in mid-week than on weekends. *Ask!*

REAL SKI BUMMING

At some ski meccas, the managers do all they can to find a staff that doesn't ski. This is understandable when you think of a big New Hampshire cafeteria, where *every* hired ski bum, including cooks, had gone off to the slopes one

Some skiers are lucky enough to live at a ski area and work there, living it up in the evening. They're known as ski bums. (Kris Rud)

All About Skiing Inexpensively

day. Or so the enraged manager claimed. "There I was, alone, faced with 2000 in for lunch. Alone! Alone!" (An aside to the ski bumming job seeker: Don't tell anyone you ski.)

The resort financiers, the people with the money satchels, can be uptight about ski bums. Managers pray for conformity, so as not to offend the middle-class customers. "A few area operators are still demanding haircuts of their employees," one ski bum says. "They're going rigid at the sight of unconventional clothing or behavior. The 'different' are being discriminated against."

One long-time observer of the ski bum scene thinks that the resorts – and the sport itself – is forever frozen at "some misty time between Herbert Hoover and Dwight Eisenhower." In an editorial, the social commentator summed it up well. "Some hip people ski. Some hip people are *in* skiing, but they hide their hipness carefully to avoid ostracism. Somewhere there is a ski area devoted to good skiing, good times, and gentle and affectionate human intercourse."

Some years ago, a now defunct ski magazine defined a genuine ski bum as the "hottest skier on the hill," as someone "who always needs a haircut, prints his own lift tickets," and is an expert at "conning drinks." When Warren Miller, the ski-movie-maker, was first hooked by the sport, he showed such survival tactics. Needing his pennies for the gas that took his ancient jalopy from one resort to another, he didn't have much money left for food. How did he eat? "I would slip into a cafeteria," he once explained. "Soda crackers and catsup are free. I'd request a little hot water and mix it with the crackers and the catsup. Result: tomato soup."

Today's young ski enthusiast belongs to another breed altogether. He or she finds a job that allows for both skiing and adequate living.

OPPORTUNITIES

If the snowfall is good, there are roughly 36,000 U.S. job openings a ski season, and the best ski bum positions, such as bartenders, high-tip waiters and waitresses, and front desk clerks with competent skills, all go fast. It is therefore crucial to show up *before* the ski season. Most insiders turn up at the resorts around Thanksgiving; this puts them (literally) on the ground floor for jobs.

Ski bums at the best resorts, like their colleagues at smaller areas, occasionally get free ski lift privileges, or at least reduced rates, specially priced season passes, and sometimes free or inexpensive lodging. They receive discounts at some ski shops and, in some cases, free insurance. You cannot count on fancy living, although a few enthusiasts even do that by becoming assistant managers of condominium apartments or by running ski lodges for absentee owners.

Opportunities exist everywhere. In Stowe, Vermont, some of the waiters and waitresses are ski bums by day and serve dinner at night. In Aspen, Colorado, scores of young fellows ski all day and then play instruments at night in the bistros. At peak periods, ski shops always need people who can help repair the complicated equipment. And any clean-cut person with a sales bend can easily find an area job selling parkas, goggles, ski racks, and other gear in ski shops or lending a hand in rental shops. Ski areas generally prefer to have women selling and checking lift tickets. What's more, ski areas usually need healthy looking individuals to place skiers on the chair lifts. Many of the loading crews are females; some manage to work just a few days a week and ski the rest of the time.

Anyone who knows how to drive a big tractor or road grader can learn to handle the big cats used for "packing" or smoothing ski slopes. Cat drivers make good hourly wages, and some of them work part-time, skiing at other times.

You can also figure that with thousands of skiers arriving, the towns need service station help, motel clerks, cooks, real estate agents, car rental helpers and so forth. If you don't mind getting your hands greasy, garage mechanics at the larger resorts are in high demand.

For people with a trade – bricklayers, electricians, cabinetmakers, carpenters, accountants – the bigger ski resorts are an open market. Some specialists can even call their own shots, i.e., they can ski whenever they want to. A whole residential section on Aspen's Red Mountain, for instance, was built mostly by ski-bum carpenters who were on the slopes when it was sunny and only appeared on the job when it snowed. According to the builders, it took three times as long to finish these fancy new buildings. But the skiers got away with it because of the labor problem. These craftspeople showed up for work at *their* convenience without getting fired.

More employment opportunities? Enterprising ski bums with a neat appearance should look into the following.

cross-country ski guide	dishwasher (many openings)
apprentice skiing instructor	unskilled area help
area photographer	motel maid
publicity release writer	hotel-motel janitor (many openings)
ticket seller	ticket checker
cafeteria help (many jobs)	general maintenance worker
bartender	busboy (many jobs)
secretary	ski repairman

How about living quarters? Some employers furnish accommodations, but ski season employees are often required to find their own. This can be difficult in the more expensive resorts. Your best plan is to arrive early in the season or before the snowfall because the bargain rooms go fast. An early comer may be able to zero in on a rented cabin, an affordable condo, or an old house. This is the smart way (and sure sign) of good ski-bumming. The savings are obvious, as long as you are in a group of four or more people. Then, unless you have a dining room job, you won't have to eat out and can eat for a few

All About Skiing Inexpensively **57**

dollars a day at "home." Even elite resorts have a few (usually run-down) houses for rent at a reasonable monthly rate. The owners expect you to stay for the winter, sign a lease, and come up with a deposit and the rent.

Naturally, there is competition for affordable housing, and you better start looking many weeks before the winter season begins. Once you are all set and snug, you can watch those first few flakes falling from the sky, with more and thicker flakes tumbling, gathering, accumulating on the slopes. Before long – Wow! – you'll be up there skiing!

SIX

Ski Fitness

SOME REASONS FOR CONDITIONING

Ski school directors, skiing instructors, athletic coaches, and physicians all agree with the National Ski Patrol and other safety-conscious organizations that you *must* be in shape for skiing. Just how fit *you* should be depends on several factors, mostly relating to your skiing ability and age. The lesser your skiing skill, the more fitness will be required.

Hal Higdon, one of the nation's prominent conditioning experts and a well-known runner, puts it this way: "When you consider the investment the average skier has in transportation, lodging, equipment, and lift tickets, it seems obvious that anything you can do to extend your time on the slope as much as one hour per day is worth doing. Or if we assume that you're going to stay up on the mountain until the lift closes, those last thirty minutes can be made more enjoyable. You won't be dragging if you are in reasonable shape."

There is an even more serious reason for getting into condition. *Without conditioning, the skier may get hurt on the slopes.* Untrained muscles just won't cope with the strain of skiing. The result can be a fracture. Weak ligaments can snap; a tense joint can be injured by a sprain in no time. In fact, physical tension is the fate of the untrained skier. Almost *every* accident survey has come up with the same results: *The under-exercised skier is in danger.*

The injury chance doubles for the beginner who *doesn't* prepare for the ski season. Whoever rests in autumn, rusts. Come winter, he or she falls apart.

But there are other reasons in favor of preparation. If you are fit, you'll enjoy a ski trip a lot more – no muscle pains, fewer stitches in your side, no exhausted stops when the downhill running gets good. In short, you'll enjoy skiing more.

These Austrian ski champions train in summer on water skis. (Hans Truoel)

Rock climbing is strenuous enough to build ski muscles. (Curtis Casewit)

BEFORE THE SEASON STARTS

Studies show that your overall attitude toward fitness has a great bearing on how well you do on the ski slopes. If you have a positive viewpoint, you won't start exercising just one day before you arrive at the area's base lodge. You will plan ahead for many weeks. You'll avoid using your automobile and walk instead. You'll try to hike at least six to eight city blocks for a starter. You'll climb the stairs on your job instead of using elevators.

Many sports-minded people get plenty of pre-season conditioning on the tennis courts. Tennis means bending, jumping, running, stretching; for this reason, steady, daily playing is considered excellent preparation for the winter. If you stick to the singles game, tennis improves not only muscle power but your circulatory system as well. Doubles can be too social and too lazy.

Mountain climbers who scale rock walls several times a week get into great shape, too, and even the weekend hiker who handles five to ten miles has achieved something for his or her ski physique. You will also enhance your fitness by cycling or jumping rope.

Golf is not considered strenuous enough, especially if you engage in it from

Ski Fitness

those ridiculous electric carts. And physical education teachers will tell you that swimming works only if you *swim* for 30 to 40 minutes. Most people, it seems, just loaf around the pool. Surfing and waterskiing, if done regularly, are excellent conditioners, although all of the above can be topped by jogging and running.

Aerobic fitness is especially important to the skier from lower altitudes who does not have time to acclimate to the rarified mountain air. Says former Olympic silver medalist Billy Kidd, "You will learn faster, ski longer, and enjoy it more if you prepare your heart and lungs before ski season starts."

If you can't stay in condition during the summer, you should at least begin preparation two months before the start of the ski season. For the average person *running for ten solid minutes every day* is recommended.

It is important to first warm up your muscles before running at full speed. This can be done by first stretching the limbs (some exercises are described at the end of the chapter). Once you have stretched, start by walking and then run slowly at a comfortable rate. Work your way up to a pace that you can sustain for the rest of the workout. A constant speed for a given length of time is more beneficial for your body than uneven spurts of fast running that leave you gasping for breath.

Running limbers you up, which is essential for skiing. It loosens you, strengthens muscles at the same time, develops your wind, and increases your stamina. After a month, the running time can be increased to 20 minutes.

Bicycling is excellent pre-season exercise. (Stott)

As a substitute for jogging, consider *daily* rope-skipping. This exercise builds coordination, strength, and stamina. Agility enhances the quick reactions which are much needed by the skier. It also increases lung power. Fortunately, rope-skipping takes little room and is, therefore, good for city people. A courtyard, a gym corner, or a large apartment room offer sufficient space.

THE GILLINGHAM SKI FITNESS TEST

Depending on your skiing skills, you can evaluate your physical condition before the snow falls. A special test was developed by John Gillingham, an Australian Physical Education Director, who made a name for himself at the YMCA. Prior to the ski season, Gillingham recommends the following "Ski Fitness" test, which can be repeated again six weeks after a proper exercise program.

PASS   FAIL

1. Run a mile without stopping. Make note of your time; ten minutes is OK, but consistent timing should bring your mile to eight minutes.
2. Hold a balance for 30 seconds, stand on tip toes, heels together, arms held out in front, eyes closed.
3. Stand feet flat with eyes closed, swing left leg at least 45 degrees forward and back five times, without losing balance. Repeat with right leg.
4. Sitting with legs together and straight out in front of you, grasp your ankles with your hands and lower head to knees. Hold five seconds.
5. Lie on your stomach with feet together (get someone to hold them) put hands behind neck and raise chin until approximately 18 inches from floor.
6. Stand, arms raised above head, feet together and flat, and slowly roll trunk down and place hands (fingertips) on floor. Keep legs straight.
7. Standing Broad Jump. Jump at least own height plus 1½ feet.
8. Lie flat on back with chin on chest, hands grasped behind neck, and legs straight. Raise feet six inches off the floor and hold for 30 seconds.
9. Hold a Wall Sit for one minute. Keep knees 90 degrees to feet and 90 degrees to hips and waist. Place back straight against the wall with arms folded.
10. Push Ups: With body straight, bend arms until chest touches floor. Do 15 times. Women may use kneeling position.

Did you pass or fail?

Ski Fitness

Note down the results, and you'll have a good clue to your current capabilities. Need improvement? If so, don't rush into a program before you have consulted a physician. She'll examine your heart; even a simple jog can drive up some people's rate to 140 heartbeats per minute. The physician will measure your blood pressure and perhaps even prescribe a diet. The less you weigh, the easier it is for your body to provide oxygen to the muscles and the easier you can ski.

THE COMPLETE SKIER'S FITNESS PROGRAM

The best way to insure that you'll get the most from your hours on the slope is to prepare your body ahead of time *for the specific stresses and strains* of this winter sport. According to one ski association physician "there are several essential areas of body tuning that even the most laid-back skier should concentrate on. First of all you need aerobic fitness for endurance. Next you need heart-lung strength, muscle strength, flexibility, and coordination."

Ski clubs, associations, and other groups often offer a fitness program before the start of the season. Inquire locally.

Certain exercises will strengthen you in each of these categories, and some will help you in more than one area. Suggestions made here can be added to and improved upon; after all, you'll want to eliminate monotony, besides tailoring the program to *your* specific needs. Besides, exercising with a skier friend (or friends) not only heightens your enjoyment of the workout, it also prepares you for the social aspects of skiing.

For the best results, begin your conditioning at least six weeks before your first run of the season. Remember to increase the duration of each exercise gradually as your fitness improves.

Each pre-season workout should begin with stretching your muscles. This will improve their reliability, later helping them to move fluidly downhill, to turn. Calisthenics prevent muscle tearing, spraining, or just "not being there" when you need them.

Some examples:

- A "trunk twist" loosens and strengthens muscles essential to those smooth, slick turns that you'll soon accomplish. Keep feet 24" apart, flat on floor, and hands on hips. Turn your trunk slowly, as far as possible left, then right.
- The "Achilles tendon stretch" is done as follows. Stand facing wall, feet together, hands flat against the wall about face high. Move feet backwards, without altering position of hands, until your body is straight and heels are barely making contact with the floor. Push down with heels till they are flat on the ground. Gradually and continuously move your feet backwards an inch at a time until the heels fail to touch the floor.
- For "inner leg stretching," stand with your legs wide apart. Bend forward until you can place your palms in front of you onto the floor approximately

three feet from your feet. Slowly bend your elbows until they are touching the mat.
- And don't forget the old-fashioned "toe toucher."

Now that your muscles are stretched, it's time to get the blood flowing. Aerobic calisthenics have become one of the most popular ways of building endurance (heart-lung capacity) and muscle strength. Aerobics involve increasing the activity of your cardio-vascular system so that your body uses oxygen faster than it can be replaced. Any exercise that makes you breathe hard will do: jumping jacks, running in place, pushups, situps, even a fast swim. Design your own set of exercises, but *keep moving* between each one so your oxygen debt is not reduced.

A few suggestions:
- Jump on one leg (your toes are bent). Alternate quickly to the other leg. Your weight should shift completely during this exercise.
- Keeping feet and knees together, hop alternately from the left to the right. Rotate your torso and shoulders as if you are skiing a slalom course.
- Jump-roping: do one-minute sets until you can last longer.

Don't forget the other activities mentioned earlier – running, swimming, cycling, perhaps even a rapid game of basketball.

MIND OVER THE MOUNTAIN

To be a complete skier, your mind and body must unconsciously work as one. As Timothy Gallway, co-author of *Inner Skiing* (Bantam, 1981) says, "Inside all of us is a mountain with no top and no bottom. The skiing there is perfect. The snow is made of pure peace and there is not a trace of Self I (your mind) interference . . . This place of perfect peace has always been within us, waiting to be sought, but it can be enjoyed only by those who have recognized the limitations of seeking this satisfaction externally."

Just getting your body into top condition is not enough to insure your success on the slopes. Instead of trying to think yourself down the hill, you must eventually achieve the confidence to let your body instinctively feel its way downhill. (You'll learn more about this in Chapter 8.)

A positive attitude is critical even for the novice. Visualize yourself confident and relaxed even if you've never been on skis! Once you're on the ski slope allow yourself to mimic, within your own mind, those skiers who are more experienced than you are. A good practice is to close your eyes and see yourself in their shoes (or, in this case, ski boots!). Skiing is not only physical but also mental.

One of the most useful and obvious helpmates is the ski school. Whether you're on skis for the first time, the second time, or the second season, you will be greatly helped by a good instructor. The next chapter tells you more about this important subject.

SEVEN

How To Find A Good Ski School

SKI LESSONS, ANYONE?

A book such as this one can get you interested in the sport, and start you off in the right direction. But no more than that. A beginner fares best by taking lessons. An intermediate can't tell how he or she looks on the slopes; it is the instructor who notices and points out the student's flaws. The non-professional teacher, although he may ski well, doesn't generally understand the whys and wherefores of skiing. Nor has he mastered the technique of instructing. The profession demands special knowledge and skills, plus experience.

Moreover, a ski school is neutral. Unlike a family member (say a husband), an instructor isn't *personally* involved. A fellow might want to assist his girlfriend, but she may consider his well-meaning corrections as criticism. She might be better off in school. An amateur teacher often demonstrates the wrong motions. Indeed, many a father has his son in tow, instructing him incorrectly, with Junior happily copying it all.

The trial-and-error method doesn't work on the slopes, just as it doesn't on the tennis court. The player who immediately learns a correct forehand, backhand, and service is ahead in the game. Some tennis buffs refuse to take lessons; such players sometimes still cannot volley or serve after five years of playing. You're in the same situation on skis.

Lessons are crucial for the first-timer, who may fumble for weeks without making any progress on his or her own. This learning process is considerably shortened with an instructor. "The first day is the most important," Jean Claude Killy once said. "And the first week in class."

Besides, you greatly reduce the chances of breaking a leg. Surveys have provided enough evidence that you are safest in a class.

Instructors will not force you to ski beyond your ability. They won't take the beginner down an extremely steep hill. They'll decrease the pace in fogs or blizzards. They'll coax the skier to better performance through demonstration. They'll reduce the number of times you fall. Groups of first-timers (who always tumble the most) can now be taught so skillfully that hardly anyone takes a spill.

Ski schools have developed scientific methods to make the student learn in record time. One of the world's best systems, the American Teaching Method, now does a superb job with beginners, using the Accelerated Teaching Method, or ATM, for short. (You'll learn details about this system at the end of the chapter.) Thanks to ATM, novices become skiers within days; individuals who are faltering, timid, or out-of-condition learn to ride the lifts after one lesson.

The next question is: How much ski school is needed? Some experts recommend that the beginner and intermediate spend five days in class, although seven would be better. Instructors will tell you that an occasional weekend class doesn't work as well as a complete course during your vacation. Naturally, one cannot make absolute rules about the frequency. This varies with a person's constitution. Some natural athletes pick up remarkable skills in a week. They have the right attitude, the sense of balance, the talent to learn new motions quickly.

So much for adults. Professional instruction is of little use before your child is four or older. Tots have a merry time in the nursery, where they may be taken outdoors for snow play. A child under the age of four has a short attention span; for this reason, the larger schools keep youngsters in special classes.

Adults tend to use their intellects, wanting to know the reason behind every movement. They don't mind listening to theory. Children, on the other hand, just want to *do* it instead, and the instructors encourage them on the slopes instead of boring them with technical language. Colorful words do the trick. "Fun" is vital, so schools for six-to-eight-year-olds concentrate on ski games. There is always one staff member, often a woman, who specializes in teaching the younger set.

Children are natural imitators and it's amazing how much they can learn in the span of a single morning if the ski school uses the "fun games" principle. A weekend instructor at one western area happens to be a young woman who teaches languages at a high school during the week. She delights her group by tossing in occasional French words, like *"Allons, mes enfants!"* At other times, she tells them, "Let's go, you tigers!" All doubts and all anxieties vanish.

Skiers often wonder if *private* lessons make sense. Group instruction is generally better for the absolute beginner. One private lesson won't do much for anyone despite the higher price. On the other hand, a series of private lessons can be a rewarding experience for an intermediate, especially with an instructor with whom you have rapport.

INSTRUCTION FOR THE BETTER SKIER

The intermediate's world grows because he (or she) can ski more trails and be able to attack different kinds of snow – layers of powder, wet, fast spring "corn," or ice. The intermediate skier will at last experience speed, which can be one of the main pleasures of the sport. When you become truly adept at this sport, you may be able to take little jumps, handle big changes in terrain, and even do freestyle acrobatics. And when you learn to ski well, there is less likelihood of an accident. One PSIA (Professional Ski Instructors of America) member puts it this way, "Lessons are in order if you can't keep up with other skiers on the mountain."

Modern North American ski schools are well organized, well controlled, and well run. A coast-to-coast study shows that small and large schools are exceedingly versatile and sympathetic to the recreational skier. Some schools have a first-rate testing system for skiers. (Directors are almost infallible – they always put the intermediate in the right class!) All over the nation, instructors attend weekly clinics where they themselves are drilled in teaching systems and kept abreast of trends.

HOW TO EVALUATE A SKI SCHOOL

Some repeat customers will travel to a certain resort, say Stowe, Vt., for the sake of its excellent ski school. Many fair skiers return for a yearly refresher course to some bastions of good teaching at Stratton, Vt., Aspen and Snowmass, Colorado; Snowbird, Utah; Killington, Vt.; and others. The beginner or less experienced skier possesses less savvy about such things and must trust the school.

How can you tell if a school is competent? There are a number of ways. First, a novice shouldn't be discouraged by sheer size. Some of America's largest schools, with as many as 250 instructors, are also the best informed and organized. Second, quality operations – as in tennis – are often headed by well-known personalities. A Director of Skiing, like Stein Eriksen (in Utah), Hank Kashiwa or Billy Kidd (both in Colorado), while not always on the school scene, will not tolerate inferior instruction. You can further rely on a school if the school chief is a member of PSIA. Such a school head will be likely to employ PSIA members, too. They are up-to-date on techniques, and their teaching standards are invariably high. Look for the PSIA insignia; consider it a guarantee of competence, meaning that the instructor has been trained and retrained to instruct. A high percentage of these pros decide to pass a certification exam, which is no small matter. The tests are so tough that in some areas less than half the candidates manage to pass.

PSIA is more than a trade association. It is also a "skiing university" for fu-

Good instructors can remember names within minutes. (Ernie Blake, Taos Ski Valley, NM)

ture professionals. The group requires no pledge of allegiance to join or no affidavit that members will use a certain method. But the instructors must reach the first-rate skiing and teaching level established by the division. Even certified teachers must attend periodic seminars and clinics.

Professional standards are equally high in the Alpine countries, especially Austria, the cradle of skiing. The Austrian National Ski School has long been under government auspices. Headquartered in St. Christoph-Am-Arlberg, the school remains as difficult to get into as a military academy. The candidates are subjected to formidable entrance exams, which include oral and written English tests, ski tests, racing tests, plus medical and police clearances. (Age limitations: 20 to 40.) After a person is admitted, he or she will face six gruelling weeks of classes that deal not only with ski teaching, but also with avalanches, rock climbing, rope techniques, basic medicine, first aid, and geology. At one point, about 15 percent of the student instructors flunk the finals.

Some schools are better than others, and some instructors are more talented,

A class should never be too large: More than ten persons are too many. (New West Agency)

of course. What's more, you'll notice innovations such as video taping. In general, even a novice can evaluate the quality of a ski school.

Here are some guidelines:

- The staff at the leading schools has been trained to check the guest's equipment. The instructor decides if the skis are suitable and the bindings are properly mounted.
- The better the school, the more division into different groups by ability. The ideal beginner classes consist of no more than ten people; intermediate classes – no more than eight; and advanced – six. You can recognize a good instructor because he or she won't play favorites; the same person will not always ski in the number-one position. (The skier following directly behind the teacher gets the most attention.) The entire class will be *skiing,* not standing around.
- The best schools employ instructors who can provide the technical guidance that allows a class member to get maximum use from the equipment. The teacher shows the way through patient demonstration, explanation, and subtle corrections of errors. (On the other hand, good ski schools make you *ski a lot,* and not just stand around). The instructor remembers names. He or she criticizes diplomatically, and avoids hurting anyone's feelings. Good instructors gladly answer questions. A nice personality is an asset, rapport an essential.
- Ski professionals will always use the existing terrain to its best advantage. The teacher will plan the descent of the class much like a coach or racer would plot a course, calculating what exercises and variations can be used on a particular hill on any particular day. Under certain snow and terrain conditions, some exercises are impractical, if not impossible. The instructor will look for the kind of terrain that will help the student execute an exercise, thus building up confidence. "The more experienced the instructors the better the ski school," says one director. "Ten years of teaching experience is one good yardstick."
- Professionals don't show off. Although they're fast, they won't ski away from the class, as they once did during pre-war days, with "Follow me!" calls. In fact, taking off has become a strict taboo for PSIA members. (You'll still find the occasional hotshot instructor in Europe, though, and classes in the Alps can be larger.) American schools make short shrift of the runaway teacher. They fire him. An instructor who is caught deserting his class at 10 A.M. may be dismissed by afternoon.

WHAT IT TAKES TO BECOME A SKIING PROFESSIONAL

Not everyone is cut out to become and remain an instructor. Some people don't have the patience; others eventually give up because they don't want

How To Find A Good Ski School 71

to teach every type of class from beginners to experts. A famous European racer, who joined one U.S. school, lasted only one year. He admitted that the job bored him.

What does it take to be on the teaching staff of a large prestigious resort? The question was asked of a ski school director who is responsible for 275 instructors at a large Colorado resort. Here's how he explained his needs: "Our philosophy is to take good skiers who are sincerely interested in working with people. They must have a talent for getting along with all types of persons and must enjoy doing so. Instructors must be neat and attractive. Because our ski school is large, they must be able to work well in an organization which is more regimented than smaller schools. We therefore require a mature, self-sufficient person who can get along with other instructors and management. We naturally look for the best qualified people."

The best qualified people include those who passed certification. The three-to-four-day PSIA certification test includes a difficult written and oral exam covering ski theory, history, psychology of teaching, biomechanics, and international rules of racing. In some regions future instructors are questioned about avalanches, too. The candidates are then brought to the snow and asked to demonstrate various ski maneuvers as clearly and precisely as possible. The would-be instructors are watched carefully and graded. Next comes the actual teaching phase. It may be the most difficult part. Each new instructor is put before a "class" composed of examiners and other experts. The applicant is asked to teach a maneuver or exercise and correct any errors he sees in his "students." Experienced examiners will attempt to confuse the candidate. But there's still more to the PSIA examination. The candidate must run a slalom course, proving he or she has complete control of his skis. Then comes the "free skiing" test, where each instructor must prove his worth with a controlled run through steep and bumpy terrain. Each major portion of the testing is graded separately, and to become certified, the candidate instructor must pass all phases. Only the best will pass.

The majority of ski teachers enjoy their winter work. They wouldn't want to be anywhere but on a ski slope. Yet they are different from the old Austrian farm boys who taught skiing in America. In recent years a new breed of American PSIA members (or ski school directors) have appeared on the scene. These people ski well, make people feel welcome, and have a college degree. This new breed knows about budgets, can read a profit and loss statement, and understands psychology.

Seasoned ski schools know what the customers want. Here are some fascinating confidential details from one ski school in the U.S. West. Here instructors are made aware of a skier's basic human motivations. Among them:

Fun . . . (Personal enjoyment.) Games on skis (hide and seek, king of the hill, obstacle course, tour of the mountain).

Status . . . (Personal recognition.) Ego satisfaction: awards and pins (best skier, most improved skier, best class, proficiency pins). Instructor's positive attitude and praise.

Service . . . Not just ski instruction, but satisfying your pupil's human needs in every possible way.

Skills . . . (Knowledge.) Proficiency tests, grading by physical challenge. (Student's awareness of constant, steady improvements).

Showmanship . . . Create interest in every phase of skiing through imaginative window dressing.

Sex . . . (Implicit and overt.) Lunch break, chairlift pairing, ski school party, evening assignments for instructors, etc. Moonlight ski trips. Never forget the fantastic drawing power of sex – pupil to pupil, instructor to pupil, and the whole implied but nonetheless fundamental mystique of sex in skiing.

One typical director reminds teachers: "Do everything possible to protect and increase your pupils' confidence. Without it your class members cannot learn. With growing assurance of his safety and ability he learns readily. Any instructor who allows a student to become frightened or unsure is failing badly. Use praise generously but honestly. There should be humor in ski lessons. Enjoy your class, the people in it. Use your imagination. Don't be a teaching machine. Gear your approach to your pupil according to your understanding of his personality and your observation of his skiing."

As a ski school customer, you certainly can't ask for more!

THE COSTS

Ski school instruction isn't cheap. Private lessons cost as much as the price of one or two lift tickets at an elite resort. A two-hour group lesson is only a little cheaper. This may not amount to as much as various equipment items; even a pair of quality ski gloves costs more than a day's instruction. But your investment always comes *on top* of the (often overpriced) ticket, transportation to area, and lodging. In Europe, ski lessons are at least one fourth cheaper than in the U.S.

You can prune expenses in various ways. First, take another look at the "Learn-to-Ski Week" that brought you to the resort. Instruction may be included in your package. When you pay for lessons, you'd be wise to buy more than one at a time. When you arrange for three (or more) lessons in advance, the price goes down. For example, a single lesson in Sun Valley costs a fortune, but if you register for five days, the individual rate goes down to a reasonable sum. Finally, inexpensive ski schools may be supported by civic organizations, churches, and certain clubs. You may not get very personal instruction, but the supervisors are sometimes professionals. Some organizations run their own buses.

How To Find A Good Ski School

Call your local ski shop and find out if it offers an instruction package. (Some larger sporting-goods chains do.) Or investigate the possibility of signing up for a ski school in your own *city!* Some newspapers, for example, offer a yearly instruction package at a reasonable rate. The newspapers do this as a promotion, and *your* cost is nominal. In most major population centers, classes exist for all levels of skiing. In Salt Lake City, one of the local newspapers got lots of PR mileage out of its excellent yearly program, and in Cleveland, a paper teaches skiing to thousands of people every season. If you live near Chicago, you should inquire about the ski school of a local daily. In Seattle, the city itself manages an excellent learn-to-ski week. You'll naturally have to register for these schools as soon as they're announced. Most programs fill up quickly, using a first-come, first-served basis. YMCAs, YWCAs, and ski clubs also run affordable programs.

THE SHORT SKI AS A SCHOOL TOOL

ATM is your ski school's shorthand for the American Teaching Method. For the student who starts on 140 to 150 cm skis, ATM is a shortcut to greater skill, more confidence, added safety, and a full measure of enjoyment. In brief, it means learning with shorter-than-normal skis.

Until a few decades ago, most people began their snowy adventure with heavy, awkward gear much taller than themselves. These long skis were difficult to carry and to walk on. Because of their bulk, the equipment had a mind of its own. The seven-footers could show their independence by slipping off in unpredictable directions, or worse, by tripping the unwary student. An older PSIA member recalls that, "For most beginners, ski school became an exercise in frustration, as the instructor tried to untangle his charges from the albatross-like grip of those clumsy, over-long skis." Most people spent their first day in class just becoming acquainted with the unwieldly gear's quirks and squirts. The 20 pounds of weight meant a marathon of will power and brute muscle power as the class stumbled up and down the "bunny hill." To no one's surprise, America's ski school drop-out rate was extremely high – well over 50 percent.

Speculation turned to experimentation and eventually to the development of GLM, or the Graduated Length Method. Careful testing and observation led instructors to a tradition-breaking conclusion: Long skis are necessary only when moving fast, which beginner skiers rarely do. The first short skis were cut-off versions of their big brothers.

The concept of GLM dates back to the early fifties, when teaching pioneers began to experiment with shorter-than-normal length skis. Instructors in Germany, France, and Austria did extensive work. In the U.S., an instructor named Cliff Taylor had already explored the idea after World War II. Taylor started students on three-footers, then advanced them in graduated steps of four-foot and five-foot, up to longer standard skis. After many years of testing his short ski method in places like Squaw Valley, California; Hogback Mountain, Vermont; and Loveland Basin, Colorado, Taylor discovered the following advantages:

1. An easy, relaxing way of controlling skis.
2. Quick advancement to all types of slopes in a relatively short period of time.
3. Mastery of the basic skiing principles at slow-to-moderate *safer* speeds, followed by high-speed skiing on longer skis.
4. Greater safety because short skis seldom get crossed and are less bulky.
5. Lower costs. (Short skis are expensive.)

Before GLM and ATM, various long-ski techniques often traumatized students who were told at one area they had to relearn what they were taught the week before at a different place. Now, ski schools emphasize their similarities rather

Some ski schools now use sophisticated video equipment. (Ampex)

than their differences. Snowmass' Ski School Director, Curt Chase, has said: "You render no service to a skier who has started to learn with one technique to tell him that everything he knows is all wrong and he must start afresh." Chase was among the first to be aware of the advantages of using a shorter ski to learn on. "Psychologically it is less disturbing. Without question it reduces the risk of injury."

Many technicians consider a shorter ski for the beginning skier to be one of the most important, dynamic, and imaginative innovations of the past decade. It has helped bring students to the slopes in record numbers.

Some ski schools have refined their teaching systems. The Killington Ski Area in Vermont, for instance, acquaints first-timers with the sport via a film that reduces fear. Students next learn to walk on short skis. When they become good at this, they learn to turn.

Nowadays the beginner is put on shorter skis at practically every ski school in North America. And for good reasons. Short skis *are* light, allowing you to turn with greater ease, making you look and feel more graceful. You need a minimal effort to ski. You therefore suffer fewer muscle pains.

This abbreviated equipment proves especially useful for:

- elderly novices
- fearful students
- physically feeble or uncoordinated persons
- the physically handicapped
- the out-of-shape

The biggest advantage for the broad public emerged soon enough: these skis became instant confidence-builders. Thanks to the innovation, instructors could guide hesitating intermediates over and through bumps. (Moreover, you can now *rent* short skis at most U.S. areas.)

While the majority of resorts adopted ATM, a few large schools in North America still use GLM (the Graduated Length Method). Among these resorts are Killington, Vt.; Boyne Mt., Michigan; and Aspen Highlands, Co.; which calls GLM the "accelerated ski method."

Which is the better system? Opinions vary among ski school directors. GLM is quicker, allowing you to swivel or turn after a few hours of instruction. Instead, ATM leads a skier to the wedge and wedge turns and then to longer and longer skis. Using a slightly wider track, ATM may be a sensible approach because you'll learn to buck difficult terrain and difficult conditions. Progress may be a little slower at first, but in the end, ATM knowledge may be broader.

Short skis, which someone once called "snowskates," have some disadvantages, too. These smaller versions are not as stable as long ones, and they don't track as well at high speeds.

A talented skier will eventually graduate to 175 cm or even 195 cm skis – or perhaps longer ones – and, if not, he or she can always stay on shorties. In either case, business booms, and ATM has reduced the school dropout rate. Once you start skiing, you'll probably keep skiing.

TEACHING CHILDREN TO SKI

Even the smallest child will usually find happiness in the snow. If your tot is under three, you can leave him or her in a ski nursery. The cost generally includes meals and supervised play.

Skiing, like all outdoor activity, fills a great emotional need in youngsters of all ages. Children do not walk; as every parent knows, they run! Skiing thus becomes no more than running on snow. Skiing gets a child away from the noisy, dusty, muddy pavement and back to Mother Nature. Skiing removes the youngster from the odors and horns of automobiles, and into a clean-smelling silent world. And although you can't tell a three-year-old about the bracing air and the motion's effects on his oxygen-starved lungs, or the improvement of muscle tone, any pediatrician can confirm these medical facts.

Professional instructors can provide some good advice. "A toddler should never be pushed into the sport!" This is the most important counsel by ski pros. "First get the small child acquainted with the wonders of snow."

Another instructor says: "Build a snowman with them! Let them slide down a slope on a piece of cardboard. And always keep them warm and dry." This way a child can first develop a "favorable attitude" to a ski area and to the sport itself. The ideal age for this is two and three. Frolicking outdoors can start with toboggans and saucers.

Soon enough, the child will be fascinated by seeing adult skiers. He will be tempted to try skiing, too. Can they ski if they can walk? Not always. Some tots just lack the strength and coordination until they are four or five. In any case, good weather is essential for the *first* experiments. (At the better ski schools, youngsters are rescued from the cold by being invited inside for hot chocolate and ski movies.)

One ski school director put it this way: "The first acquaintance with skiing must be made as pleasant as possible. Otherwise your child's interest may well be over."

How can the instructor speed up the initial learning process for the three-to-four-year-old? Small children are great imitators, and expert ski teachers always play some sort of game with them. Skiing to pre-schoolers should be all games, all joy. Some of the games involve slalom poles or ski poles.

Most large ski centers nowadays have specialized, diversified children's programs, run by *specialized* instructors, in many cases, by young, enthusiastic women who like kids. U.S. family resorts like Mount Snow, Vt.; Hunter Mountain, N.Y.; or Winter Park, Co.; have especially well-developed children's programs. Winter Park actually has a special mini-mountain, "Penguin Peak," for youngsters ages three to four, and a "Gnome Forest," where only kids are al-

Certain parents are able to teach their own youngsters, but this isn't always the case. (Utah Travel Council)

lowed. Barbara Roylance, the supervisor of these programs (which include ages five to eight and eight to thirteen), explains the basic philosophy: "Kids here must have a good time. That's paramount. Of course, outgoing young persons do better than the introverted ones. And the child should be physically fit."

John Alderson, a well-known children's instructor, sums it all up this way: "In a kids' class, or any class for that matter, I let that part of me forward that loves to play, and wrap it around my wealth of skiing knowledge in a type of Teacher's Sandwich. To them I'm just an over-sized, enthusiastic kid with lots of crazy and fun ideas on what to do and where to go. So through constructive play and soft competition (play hard, play fair, nobody hurt), I find kids learn to ski, and love it."

EIGHT

Learning To Ski In Record Time

FIRST STEPS

Thanks to ATM in the U.S. and the shorter ski all over the world, ski schools manage to teach even non-athletic people at a fast pace. The slopes are now superbly groomed; instruction systems have been simplified and streamlined. When you watch instructors demonstrating their national techniques at various international "Inter-Ski" meetings, you won't detect many differences between the various schools. Skiing has therefore become less difficult to learn than it used to be, particularly in the U.S. where thousands of PSIA professionals keep you from floundering.

Ready to head for the school meeting place?

The first step is carrying your own gear. It's important to carry equipment correctly because the gear could hit someone, or slip out of your grasp and be damaged. Skis should not be held in the arms or under the arms. Instead, the skis belong on your shoulders, tips forward. This isn't hard if you place them bottom to bottom. Pick either shoulder and slide the poles under the skis for support. Now you hardly feel the weight of your equipment. If you must walk in a crowd, pay attention to the backs of your skis.

It is time to step into the bindings. If possible, have an instructor look over the release mechanism. All skis feel alien at first, but you get used to them quickly. Eventually this equipment will be part of you, an extension of your body.

Don't be disappointed if your class stays at first on flat terrain. This makes sense, so that you can get the feel of your gear. To start with, your instructor

This photo shows how easy it is for beginners to learn on short equipment. (Killington Photo)

will have you walk a little on level ground. Actually, this isn't more difficult than normal walking. The trick? Keep sliding and take small steps. Push yourself alternately with the right and left ski pole. And while you're on the level, remember *not* to lift your skis. Gliding involves less effort.

Presently some instructors may lead the class to a short hill and show them how to *schuss*, i.e., to slide straight down. Other instructors may insist that you sit on the snow in order to learn how to get up again. Well, beginners do fall often, especially when they're not in class. They can fall and look like pretzels, and if the first-timer ventures into deep snow – which he shouldn't – he can look as white as a snowman. If you're in good condition, a fall is not dangerous, and even the hard-packed snow is softer than pavement.

The important thing is never to strain against a fall. Let go; tumble lightly and try to come down sideways onto your hips or your behind. Try to keep your skis together so that they don't scissor.

How do you get up again? The teacher will demonstrate how to move the skis into a horizontal position. (If the tips point down a mountain you'll slide hopelessly downward!) After the feet are side by side across the slope, the experienced getter-upper makes one unit out of the two poles, which are placed upright into the snow. Hold onto the baskets with one hand; the other goes on the pole grip. Some rocking and an upward push may suffice. You are in a standing position once more. The getting up part can be a little more difficult for the novices or the overweight, but it's good exercise, anyway. If the poles don't work, there's no law against using your gloved palms instead.

Learning To Ski In Record Time

CLIMBING, SCHUSSING, TURNING

At this point, not all American schools follow the same teaching sequence. Unlike their European counterparts, American professionals are less dogmatic and are given a wider latitude in what to do next. Some schools will leave out certain exercises on which others insist, and most instructors adapt their sequence to the students' collective ages and skills, as well as to weather and slope conditions. On certain days you may be skiing more instead of watching demonstrations; on other days, an instructor may want you to listen for ten-minute stretches.

After teaching you walks on the level and getting up, some instructors may want to teach you how to complete a circle on flat ground by stepping around. Place your feet parallel, feet together. Now transfer all your weight to one ski, and swing the tip of the unweighted ski around. Now transfer your weight again, and bring the tip of the stationary ski around so that it is next to the first ski. Continue in this manner and you can complete a circle, or a "wagon wheel," as some people call it.

Once you're equipped to slide smoothly on flat terrain and change direction, you'll be ready for a short uphill hike. The easiest way is by sidestepping.

Many ski schools do especially well with children who are grouped in various classes by age. (Jackson Hole, WY)

Instructors compare this to climbing a set of stairs *sideways*. The maneuver is simple. Plant your poles for support. Lift your uppermost ski above the ground and put it down a foot higher up the mountain. Now let the lower ski follow until your two feet are side by side again. Of course, you can only do this by remaining horizontal to the slope. Take small steps. You will be told that the skis must be parallel at all times. Don't get them crossed!

The "herringbone" is another (and a little more strenuous) way to get uphill. Few schools insist on teaching it because alpine skiing has pretty much eliminated climbing. But the herringbone technique *is* useful for the more ambitious wilderness-oriented skiers. Once off the trail for a forest picnic, you may encounter an uphill stretch, and you'll be glad to know this trick. The system also works on cross-country skis.

The herringbone was named after the ski track left in the snow: it looks a little like a fish bone. Try the maneuver on a gentle slope first, and then graduate to a steeper one. Plant the poles behind you and spread your ski tips, to form a "v." The steeper the slope, the more you must part your skis. When you move upward, you can use your inside edges like long knives that slide into the snow. Ready? Try the right ski first: lift it, and still wide-angled, take it upward and come down on the inside edge. Bring your right pole up, making sure that your poles are always behind your bindings, thus supporting your weight. Now the left ski goes up, and the left pole follows.

What's the most frequent mistake of first-timers? They get the tails crossed. Remedy? Aim the ski high enough. And always remember an important rule: the poles must support you!

The herringbone can be tiring, but there is one consolation. When you learn how to use the lifts – and you will soon! – you will no longer have to climb under your own steam. Maybe that's why humorist Mort Lund describes the herringbone as "climbing up the trail hastily in an awkward attempt to retrieve a lost hat . . ."

What goes up must come down. Unless they have already done so, your ski guides will now introduce you into the thrills of the first "schuss." (It stands for "shot," which applies to a racer's rocket-like downhilling.)

Downhill running doesn't require great courage if the slope is easy. Keep your ankles, knees, and torso flexed. The feet are slightly apart for added balance. Let your shoulders remain slightly ahead of your hips. The legs must be supple during the descent. Stay loose! As you ski, relax your hands and arms. You'll soon discover that it makes sense to keep the weight in the middle and on the arch of your feet. Many beginners make the mistake of leaning back. You will also learn how to adjust the downhill position to the terrain. An instructor will remind all *schussers* that the steeper the grade, the more forward you lean. Naturally modern boots help you adjust to the terrain – emphasis is now more on balance.

Now that you've been taught to handle a first downhill run, you will be taken

Learning To Ski In Record Time **83**

to a somewhat steeper slope. If you were to zip down in a straight line, the laws of gravity would make you go fast. This direct route is called "skiing the fall line."

A traverse is a better idea. It simply means crossing the slope at a slightly downward angle, or, to use another term, handling a slope obliquely. (The dictionary defines oblique as: "neither perpendicular, nor horizontal, but slanting," or "not direct in descent.") Your instructor will explain that the slow journey across a hill controls your speed.

Although it seems unnatural, you'll be shown to keep your weight *away* from the slope while traversing. The steeper the terrain, the more weight goes on the uphill edge of your downhill ski, which is the one that looks down the hill. The downhill shoulder and the hips are bent slightly toward the valley for bal-

A first downhill schuss for the novice. Note the knees. (WP)

ance. The uphill ski is somewhat ahead. Beginners often reverse the process, lose their balance, and start slipping. Incidentally, your knees should also move in the direction of the hill. This will tilt the skis on their edges and give you a better purchase on the slanted terrain. By using your edges you will travel down the mountain in a traversing line. Now try to reduce the amount of edge pressure by moving your knees straight up! This motion releases your edges. Gravity takes over.

Watch the teacher. His or her skis will begin to slip downhill in a lateral (sideways) direction. This is called "side slipping." It doesn't indicate a loss of control, but is done on purpose. Side slipping may come in handy on very steep slopes. The instructor can actually sideslip straight down the fall line, i.e., the steepest downhill line of a long slope. You merely relax your edges, forbidding them to cut into the slope. When you want to stop, make the edges grip once more.

THE GLIDING WEDGE

After you learn how to go up, down, and across, you must learn how to slow down. Beginners do this by plowing the snow with their skis. A snowplow looks like the Cadillac sign or a "V," and was renamed some years ago "the wedge." It is good preparation for the first turns, too. Your ski tips are almost, but not quite, together. (Instructors don't want to get them crossed.) As always, the knees are slightly bent. The skis remain flat as you slide downhill. Try to distribute your weight on both skis, if possible. (Beginners often look lopsided when they try their first wedges.)

You hold the poles at about hip level, with the baskets behind you. The small v slows you down, and if done correctly, should bring you to a complete stop. It works well on short skis.

Practice the (narrow) gliding wedge and the braking possibilities of the wider wedge first on a gentle slope. It is less exhausting that way. If you're not skiing in class, you should avoid unpacked slopes for this maneuver. Powder snow makes it harder to learn.

PSIA ski schools swear by the gliding wedge. One director gives some good reasons for using this approach:

- The gliding wedge supplies the student with a solid triangular base.
- The gliding wedge introduces the brushing-sideslipping use of the edges, without abandoning the triangular base of the wedge.
- The wedge can be used as a braking maneuver.
- Turning becomes simple, unstrenuous, and can be performed without abandoning the triangle position.
- While performing this rudimentary maneuver, the student learns lasting concepts of ski mechanics: steering, weight transfer, edge control, independent leg action.

The wedge, also known as the snowplow. (WP)

Indeed, the gliding wedge will soon lead to the first turns. The gliding wedge turn (formerly known as the snowplow turn) lets your legs steer in any chosen direction. You can do this with any length of skis, and when your instructor demonstrates the turn, you'll marvel at the stability and balance. You'll soon reach some skill with this maneuver, which is not especially difficult or complicated.

You begin in a narrow wedge (or snowplow) position and achieve the steering with your outside foot. As you turn the ski, you'll turn your body as well, which puts you into a new direction. No violent tilting motions! No extreme leaning out!

Your position is only important as it relates to your balance. American instructors will ask for a relaxed and natural stance. Your weight should be centered, perpendicular to the slope, and equally distributed over the arches of both feet. This relaxed position is familiar and easy to achieve.

A word about your arms. In the initial turns, many professional instructors prefer that you let your arms hang limply to the side with the poles bouncing behind. (The use of poles comes later; this way you learn only one thing at a time.) When the steering movement is mastered, your hands will come up and eventually assume their correct level, slightly ahead of the hips.

The class will gradually ski faster and on steeper hills. Your instructor now adds another element, the knee, to your simple steering action. Here is the real secret to modern skiing. To enhance the turning action of the ski, the student pushes the outside knee forward and toward the direction he wishes to go. Turning left thus means steering with the right knee. You push it forward and move it internally to the left, that's all. Some beginners make uneven turns because of trying *too* hard; contorting the body and thrashing for a pole plant. In time you'll learn to relax, keeping your knees bent and your hands ahead of you as you curve into a turn. Some schools help you to improve by visualizing, analyzing, and even by means of written reports.

ONWARD, UPWARD, DOWNWARD

These steered turns and various wedges will eventually lead toward the goal of many skiers: the parallel turn on any terrain. Some schools move on rapidly to this achievement; some insist on various transitions like uphill christies or wedge christies (named after Christiania, a town in Norway).

Instructors used to dwell briefly on non-related items such as skating steps or kick turns, for example. The American Ski School System doesn't endorse the latter, hoping to get you downhill in a more elegant fashion. On the other hand, the kick turn allows you to handle impossible conditions, such as steep *rocky* slopes, deep snow or ice. Kick turning is done from a standing position, most often on ultra-steep slopes, where the student does not dare to make a wedge turn. You might call it an "emergency exit." Certain ski schools around the world still teach this direction change as a solution for the "psyched" skier. Other instructors shy away from this more advanced maneuver; they feel that it's not safe for a beginner. The ability to kick turn makes sense for those who ski on difficult and unpacked ski slopes of the Alps.

Try it initially on a slight incline until it becomes easy.

First place your skis directly across the fall line so they don't slip when you're in the middle of the trick. Your poles should be planted a little ahead and to the side of your body. Put all your weight on your uphill ski, and swing the downhill ski (as if you were kicking a ball) so that the rear is placed in the snow and your ski sticks straight up.

Next plant your downhill pole behind you, above the uphill ski, and let your downhill ski swivel around and land on the snow. At this moment, your skis are facing opposite directions. This may seem awkward at the beginning. You'll have no trouble if you position yourself directly across the fall line, though. Now put all your weight on the downhill ski, lift the uphill ski off the snow and swing it around to where it faces the new direction.

The kick turn will permit you to ski diagonally across the slope, or traverse, and then change direction and ski across the slope the other way.

The path to skiing competence generally leads to the parallel turn.

A parallel turn is achieved by employing only your feet and knees, which steer, not slide, the skis. At all times, your upper body remains relaxed and quiet. When done correctly, it actually takes a minimum of effort to change direction. The expert's turn looks like one single, smooth movement. The American Teaching Method no longer insists on skis (and knees) kept tightly together. You ski with feet apart, which makes for better balance, too.

At first, gentle terrain will serve as your teaching and practice area for the parallel turn. Some schools may ask you to discard the poles for a short time so that you can concentrate fully on the lower portion of your body. Somewhat later, pole action will be added to increase your rhythm and to initiate your turn.

Your confidence will increase with what the instructors refer to as mileage. After awhile on the slopes *without falling*, you can "psych" yourself to make a lot of progress. Soon, you will feel comfortable steering with both feet, knees, and skis. As both legs move toward the intended direction change, the skis will become a single unit. The outward push of the knees, the momentum, and the shape of the skis themselves will contribute to easy turns.

You will be most at ease with skis about ten inches apart, and you will begin to "carve" instead of slide through the turn. The more knee action, the more stability and control. If your legs are able to move independently in response to terrain changes, a sense of balance is achieved. This is the age of the linked turn; parallel classes no longer traverse the whole slope between turns. Instead, they ski directly down the fall line in a series of quick swivels: the end of one turn is the beginning of the next. Acceleration helps, of course, and increases your grace and precision.

In most ski schools, the turn is achieved by unweighting. The skier's body comes up for an instant. Your skis are now almost weightless. You slide them around in a half circle and complete the turn. The higher the speed, the less uphill motion. The rising and sinking motions are actually combined with an ankle, knee, and waist flex.

Many ski technicians initiate the parallel turn by means of compression. This is the opposite of unweighting. At the crucial moment, you go *down*, bending the knees and the hips in the direction of the turn. This causes the skis to hold an edge. As you complete a turn, weight is then applied to the uphill ski to begin the next compression. Ski racers often make a quick step up onto the uphill ski which enhances the carving motion.

It should be emphasized that you don't master parallel technique fully until you can make fast, aggressive turns on extra steep, rugged slopes. Don't feel badly about this. Steep terrain can even cause problems to some instructors. Some time ago, for instance, the PSIA held its certification exams on the toughest imaginable slopes in Montana. The would-be instructors were first asked to complete smooth parallel turns on the intermediate slopes. After they did beautifully, they were asked to make the same perfect turns on brutally steep moguls. Several instructor candidates failed.

The above may be of interest to the average skier as well. Advanced parallelling requires a first-rate physical condition. You also need good coordination, timing, and good reflexes. Most of these can be acquired through patient, repeated instruction and practice.

You obviously can't consider yourself an accomplished skier until you can handle any gradient. Being afraid of steepness means hesitating, and you won't be able to synchronize your motions. How can the problem be overcome? Ski in an easier class; learn to handle steep short stretches straight down, and become a better intermediate skier. Then go back to the parallel forms. Keep trying. When you finally do it you'll be rewarded. You are now an advanced skier!

ADVANCED SKIING

Advanced skiing opens new horizons. It enables you to enjoy yourself more and to *relax* on the slopes. You can finally handle any terrain with ease and brag about it afterwards during the aprés-ski hour.

The ability to absorb big bumps efficiently becomes a necessity for advanced skiing. Let's say you're going very fast. You turn a corner and – surprise – run smack toward some moguls. If you hit them full blast, you find yourself thrown into the air. A landing would probably mean a wipe-out and perhaps even an injury. So you had better absorb the bump.

There are many ways to do this, depending on your speed. If you are moving very fast, you can pre-jump the mogul. This is a method used by downhill racers. The object of a pre-jump is to leap *before* you hit the crest. Let a racer show you how. Notice the accurate timing. The racer knows in advance where to take off.

A skier who travels at lower speeds can absorb the impact of a bump by using the knees as shock absorbers. The skier can bend up or down, depending on the type of terrain. To do this consistently, you should be in good shape.

An expert should be able to ski in all kinds of snow conditions, from deep fresh powder to ice. Let's first look at the more pleasant of the two.

Skiing powder is like being in another world, floating up and down, back and forth, like surfing or flying through the sky in a motorless glider. Powder yields the ultimate ski experience. Ski schools teach how to ski it in the West.

You usually begin on an intermediate slope. You must be completely relaxed and in a fearless frame of mind. The kind of light snow that falls in dry climates like Colorado or Utah requires only minor adjustments to the parallel technique. You merely stand in the middle of your skis and remain loose, with the weight evenly on both skis. How about heavy wet powder? It would be

A skier's ultimate aim is the perfect parallel turn. **(Eaton, Waterville Valley, NH)**

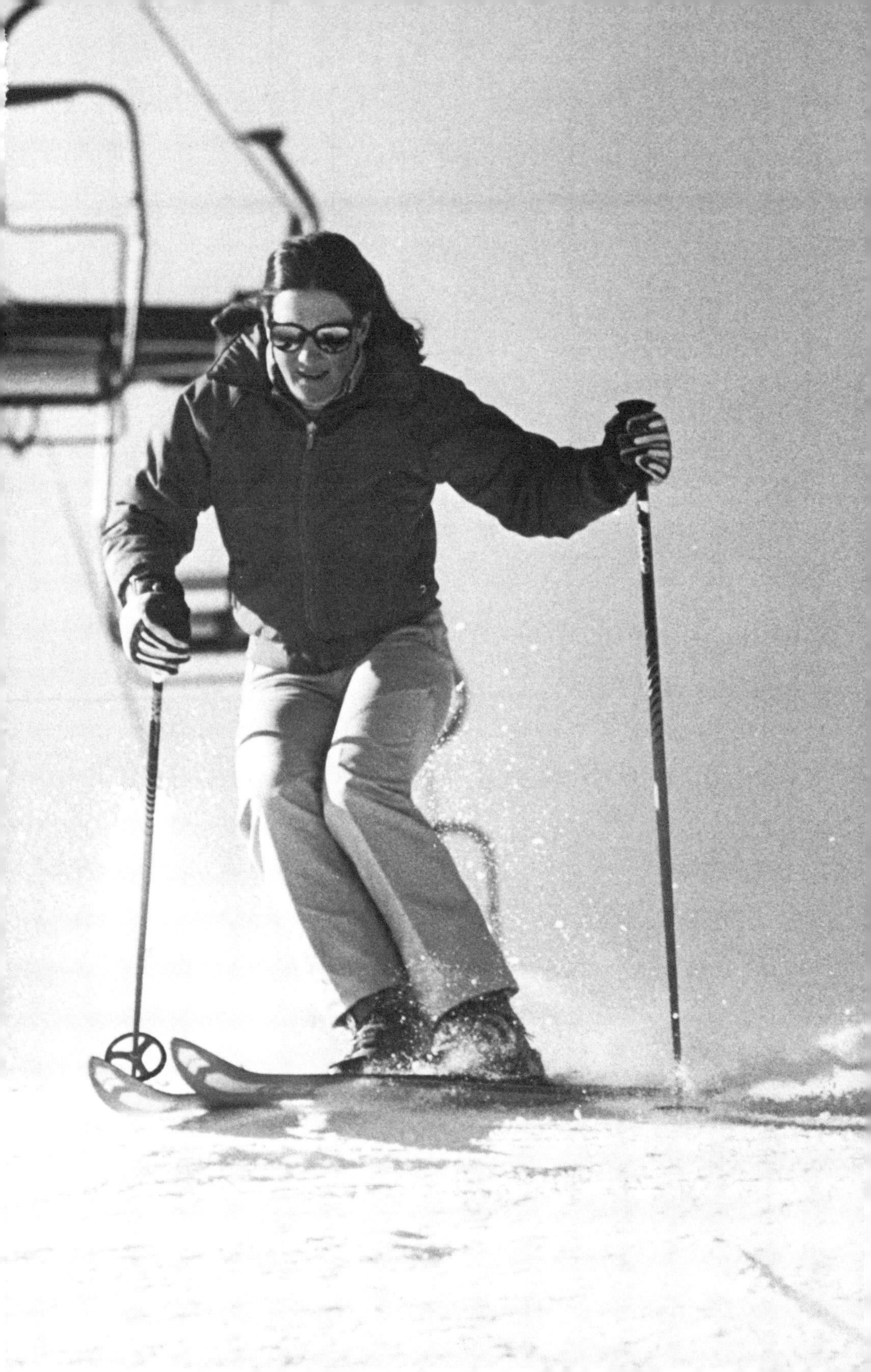

helpful if you were in good condition because the snow's extra weight requires leg strength.

One method of skiing heavy powder means that you lean back more on your skis. This enables you to turn more easily by reducing tip friction. (Many beginners keep their weight so far forward that their tips dig into the snow.) The deeper and heavier the snow, the further you lean back, but as always, your upper body remains static.

Once you've done a successful series of parallel turns in the deep feathery stuff, you'll want more of the same. You're off the trail and in another, much quieter world. You can stop and study your tracks: you've carved your own style into this slope.

If you live in the East, you'll regularly face icy trails and runs. So you'll have to develop confidence and the necessary ice tactics. Short patches will give you no trouble. You can just ski across them. Keep a straight course with your weight well over the skis. But what about an entire ice slope? Better skiers avoid the sideslip. More important, the expert doesn't freeze up, but keeps turning to slow his speed. The forward bend and angulation of the ankles is emphasized. So is the weight on the downhill ski. The edges should bite, and to do so, they must be sharp.

For "breakable crust," actually a cover of hard snow on a deeper layer of soft snow, caution is in order. Here you must be light on your skis, and do a minimum of edging.

Corn snow is generally found in spring after freezing and thawing. It is granular like sugar and feels best during the morning when the sun's melting action has just set in. This type of snow can be delightful because it's very fast; besides, in spring you wear less clothing and your movements are much more free. The mushy variety of corn is less pleasant, and takes some strength. Most people stay clear of it, judging from the empty slopes at 3 P.M. on certain April days.

NINE

The ABC's of Ski Lifts and Some Safety Rules

First-timers are often taken to a ski lift after a few hours of instruction. Don't fear. These mechanical contraptions are not difficult to use. At most areas, the operators always stand by to help you, and they slow down the machinery for novices or children. Riding instructions are posted at every loading platform. If you are unsure, ask the attendant for assistance. While you wait in line, watch others and observe how they get on.

This interesting conveyance can be found in Vermont. (Mount Snow, VT)

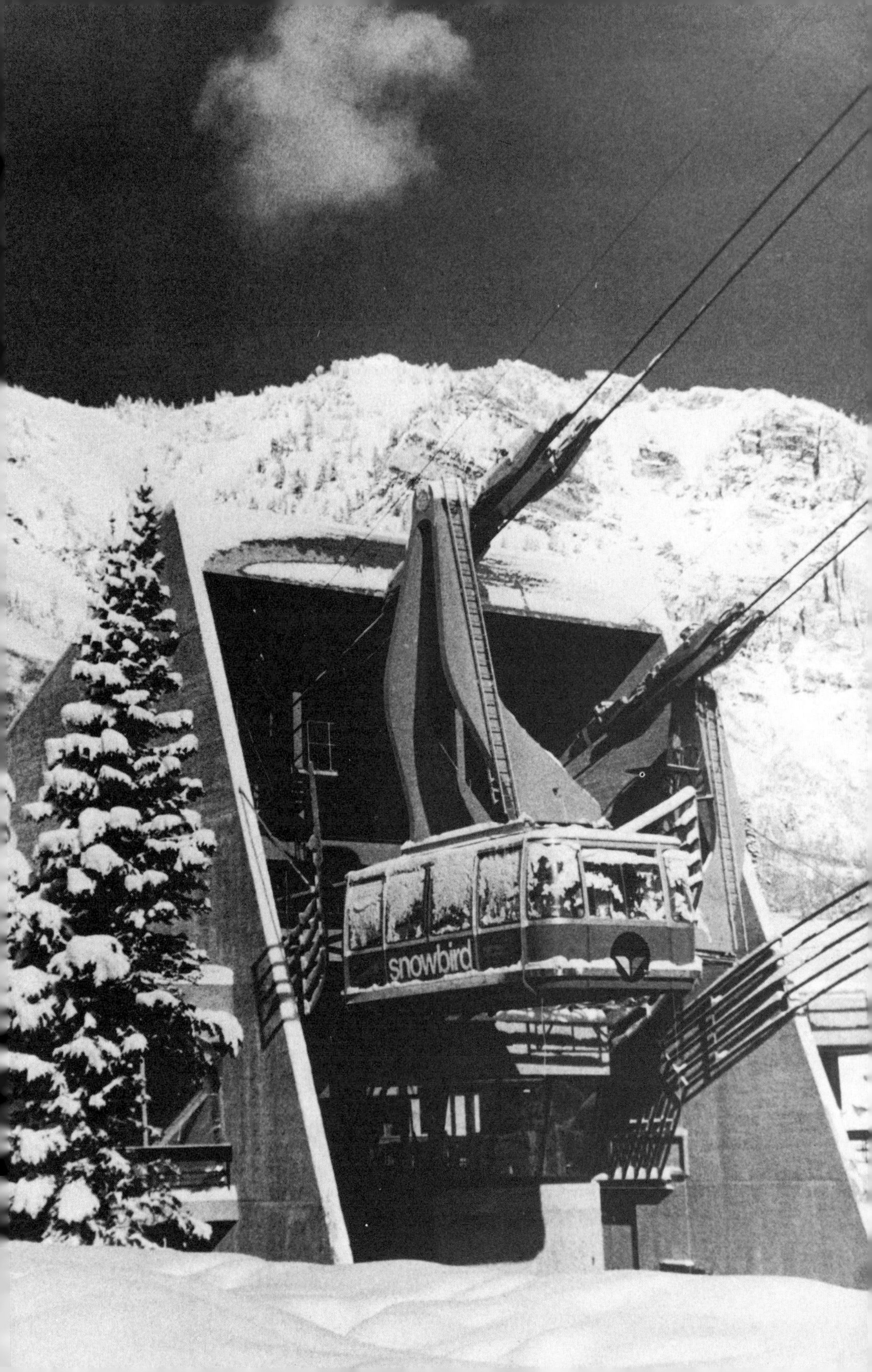
snowbird

The ABC's of Ski Lifts and Some Safety Rules   **93**

Although lift-caused accidents seem rare for intermediate and expert skiers, the exceptions are always people who don't pay attention. Recently, two boys were engrossed in talk as they stood waiting for the uphill ride at a western area. They didn't look at the double chair, which knocked them down like bowling pins. Likewise, skiers sometimes stand directly under a moving lift chair and get hit

Ski lifts are safe, according to *Ski Area Management Magazine,* which has made many studies and collects statistics on the subject. Even machine-caused freak accidents are rare. The U.S. Forest Service, various "Tramway Boards," and other supervisory agencies watch over the mechanical safety; there are also many inspections by each state.

There are many ways to get to the top. Helicopters ply the Canadian and U.S. Rockies. Tramways zoom up mountains at speeds of 30 miles per hour with computer-directed "fail safe" systems. Most chairlifts transport some 800 to 2,000 skiers per sixty minutes. And with *many* units operating at the same time at the better ski areas you generally get your money's worth, despite high ticket prices.

TRAMWAYS

Tramways, also known as cable cars, are large box-like contraptions that can hoist masses of customers – as many as 160! – to remote peaks in record time. "Jigback" cable cars ascend the German, French, and Swiss mountain giants; you'll also find these costly, convenient trams at such places as Jay Peak, Vt.; Cannon, N.H.; Jackson, Wyoming; and Heavenly Valley, California, to name a few. A Swiss-built wonder tram at Snowbird, Utah, loads almost 1000 people per hour, doing an 8000-foot trip in six minutes.

Skiers on both sides of the Atlantic often prefer trams to other forms of locomotion. There is usually room for 80 to 120 people and the ride is smooth and fast. You also won't be exposed to the elements.

The disadvantages are minor. You'll have to take your skis off after each run, which you may want to do in some areas, anyway. At Davos, Switzerland, for instance, the Parsenn tram allows you to ski one of Europe's longest runs, which may keep you busy all morning. These cable cars cannot operate under severe wind conditions, so you can't ride them all the time. A final problem is that because of their popularity, tramways generally attract the longest lift lines. (A solution is to use the same resort's chairlifts instead, and at some places ticket prices are reduced for non-tram skiers.)

Contrary to the jokes, no tram towers have ever collapsed and no cars have ever jumped off the tracks. Nor are such events likely to happen. Each tram

Tramways have the advantage of carrying many people. But you must take your skis off. (Snowbird Ski Resort, UT)

A gondola usually seats four people. (Killington, VT)

usually has a braking system on top of its track, which grips the steel cable and holds the cabin in place in case of an emergency. Some tram towers can be as high as 15-story buildings. Haul line cables may have a breaking strength of 78 tons. At one Wyoming installation it would take 232 tons to snap the track cables. Down in the valley, at the station, you notice cement counterweights that weigh from 80,000 to 160,000 lbs. That's enough safety for anyone.

GONDOLAS

Gondolas, despite their egg shapes, could be the tramways' little brothers (or sisters). Gondolas also shield you from the wind and shut down under severe conditions. In most cases, you must take off your skis for the ride. You can also take the weight off your feet – the cabins seat from four to six people. (In Switzerland a few gondolas seat two.) At some modernistic installations – a typical one operates at Steamboat Springs, Colorado – the doors lock automatically and the machinery is super-sophisticated. (The Steamboat lift has 99 cabins, by the way, and can handle 1200 people per hour.) Gondolas are in great demand by North America's skiers. Some resorts manage to forge ahead and overtake their competitors because of gondolas. At one Vermont area, there exists a gondola for the ultra-lazy skier. The cabin takes you all the way up with your skis on your feet!

With proper maintenance, gondolas operate safely. The exceptions, such as Vail's catastrophic accident in 1976, are rare. This accident was caused by one of the support cables unraveling 125 feet above the ground. The unfortunate result was that several gondolas crashed, killing and maiming numerous people and keeping the courts busy with multi-million-dollar lawsuits.

CHAIRLIFTS

While still not as numerous in Europe as they should be, chairlifts are the most popular uphill conveyances in North America. The investment is high. In the West, for instance, where slopes are long, a ski area must shell out $300,000 to $800,000 for a lift and installation. Double chairlifts allow a skier to ride up with a companion, and strangers often get acquainted that way. Single chairs (for only one person) still run at some resorts in the Alps. But the fashion has turned against the single chair, particularly in America, where skiers are wooed and pampered by the industry. To speed up the flow, some progressive resorts have installed *triple* chairs, and there are even chairs that seat four!

Although you can only bounce your legs, a chairlift ride isn't as cold as you might think; two people always shield one another from the wind. In addition, to protect you from cold seats areas use soft styrofoam seats.

You'll find it easy to use a chairlift. Grab your pole shafts in one hand, watch the chair as it approaches, and just sit down. Timing is important. If in doubt,

The first chairlifts were improvised, like this historic one, which resembles a barber chair. (Sun Valley News Bureau)

Typical double chair is now the mainstay of America's lift machinery. (Heavenly Valley, CA)

just observe the skier ahead of you. There is a lapse of several seconds between chairs, giving you enough time to get on without trouble. Mishaps are rare, but bad timing can cause a fall. Sometimes the rider doesn't keep the ski tips up, which get stuck in the platform or in the snow, upon loading, or during the ride up. The result is a wipeout. A third problem occurs when the skier horses around or jumps down somewhere along the route, which is forbidden. (You must wait until you reach the top.) In recent years, chairlifts have been built much higher above the ground, which makes a leap more difficult and often impossible.

A final note on getting off the chair. Steep summit ramps are common. Beginners should push off the chair and immediately lean forward with bent knees. It is important to get quickly out of the way of other skiers. There is no reason for anxiety; if you fail to leave the chair on the summit, the machinery will take you around and then down again.

Only a tiny minority of skiers suffer phobias when it comes to these uphill conveyances. Perhaps they were stuck on a disabled lift for thirty minutes, or even forced to evacuate by means of ropes tossed by the Ski Patrol. Perhaps they've read about accidents. Luckily, your pharmacist can come to the rescue. A phobia can often be eliminated with a tranquilizer drug.

T-BARS

A T-bar lives up to its name. It has a cross bar, which looks like a reversed "T." An operator places the wooden pole under your seat. You and your partner lean lightly against it (don't try to sit on it), hold onto a center bar, feel a little starting jerk, and presently slide upward. Don't try the T-bar the first time on skis, though. Your legs still won't be able to cope with the unevenness of the terrain, which can be rutted.

The T-bar has become a rarity at the larger resorts in North America but some area operators, notably in Europe, still favor this contraption. It doesn't cost much to install and, depending on length, can transport 800 to 1000 persons per hour. New skiers show less fondness for T-bars. One drawback is that people of different heights – an adult and a child, for example – must make awkward adjustments to ride together.

T-bars demand some alertness. You must look over your shoulder as the contraption arrives. On an undulating uphill route, you must remain as flexible as though you were skiing downhill. A "look-no-hands" trip can result in a loss of control, which can bring the entire machinery to a stop. (If you fall, get out of the way of other people at once!) Beginners often make the mistake of using the crossbar as if it were a chair. You need merely *lean* against it – don't sit on it. Keep your legs apart on the uphill trip.

T-bars were built for two people, and some extra-busy areas insist that you travel with a partner. If you need a partner, call "single!" and you'll often find

Closeup shows that you don't sit on a T-bar; you lean against it. (Swiss National Tourist Office)

A poma lift pulls up the individual skier. While still found in the Alps, this conveyance has become rare in North America. (Swiss National Tourist Office)

A rope tow is almost impossible to find in the United States. (Swiss National Tourist Office)

someone of the opposite sex. On a quiet day, however, you may have to ride the T-bar alone. The "solo" technique is to use both hands. One hand goes to the edge of the crossbar; the other holds on to the center pole. Your body should be as close to the center as possible. Carry your ski poles in your outside hand.

Although they have become unpopular in the U.S., T-bars have one great advantage. If the machinery fails, you're not stuck ten meters above the ground, as on the triple chair. Instead you're on *terra firma*. Wherever you are, you can take off and head for the valley!

POMA LIFTS

A Poma lift works on the same principle as the T-bar except that it loads only one person at a time. A round dish, or platter, takes the place of the "T." That's why these lifts are sometimes called "platter-pulls." Named after its inventor, Pomas are cheap enough to erect and can transport 400 to 1000 skiers per hour, depending on the slope length. A long steep Poma (known as *Schlepplift* in the Alps) is less than ideal for first-time skiers. They can be fast and abrupt, with tricky loading. The bumpy upward terrain can trip up a weak skier, who should first try the smallest, shortest poma available.

The safety-conscious American ski areas usually employ operators to assist you. Unfortunately, this is no longer the case in the Alps. Here you'll encounter more and more self-service platter lifts.

To use a Poma lift, squeeze the round seat between your legs, pull the lever, hold on to the bar, and go. Expect a rude start. An instructor says, "Stay loose. Remember that a tense body actually fights against this type of pull-lift. On the other hand, a relaxed person adjusts to unexpected forces." Pomas have become rare in North America, but you'll still see them at smaller ski areas.

ROPE TOWS

If you skied before World War II in the U.S. or Europe, you used mainly rope tows. At one time, this was the only way to get up a hill. They are mentioned here only for historical interest.

Rope tows take some muscle strength because you reach the top only by holding on to the rope. Fortunately, the few existing rope tows are found mostly on children's slopes or as a connection between other lifts. If you're faced with one, grasp the rope with one hand in front of you and keep the other hand behind you, squeezing the rope under your arms. Never wear loose clothes or a scarf when riding such a conveyance. There is no need for apprehension; customers are *not* swallowed by the summit machinery. A safety device releases automatically if you travel beyond a certain point.

The first rope tow, Woodstock, Vermont. (Suicide Six, VT)

SKI COURTESY (AND SOME TRAFFIC RULES)

Skiing has its own etiquette. It demands that you wait your turn in the lift line. Instructors with classes may cut the lines. If you're alone, you can call for a partner. Once on top, you'll have to observe other niceties and common sense rules. The beginner has no more business speeding than an average motorist has to enter an Indianapolis auto race. "Beginners still don't know how to use their brakes," says one ski area operator. "They blast downhill and can't stop. That's why some 55 percent of breaks happen to novices!"

The rules of the ski roads are easy to grasp. The pistes (runs) demand the same courtesy as our super-highways. In fact, at the big areas, ski runs *are* turnpikes. If you reach them through a small side path, you must stop and wait until the road is clear.

Once on the trail, keep to the right. The speedier skier behind you is responsible, just as is the driver in the rear. Prudent skiers observe their distance. If you do overtake someone, don't yell, "Track!" Instead, call, "On your left!" (or "On your right!") This tells the other person where you're passing. When you zoom past, leave plenty of space for the slower skier; otherwise, the overtaken skier can get hurt. (Think of a car that is forced off the road and goes into a ditch.)

While the fast individual has a responsibility, the slow person or stopped one has responsibility, too. Never wait in the middle of a busy ski run, or you may suffer the fate of a driver who parks in the middle of a highway. And never stand where those above you can't see you. The *edge* of the run is always safer for a rest. There is less of a risk for collision. If you fall on a major ski run, try to pull your ski to a horizontal position. Then get up, and if you must rest, stay on the *side* of the course.

Although the expert may go fast and do some joyful jumping, he or she should *always be prepared to stop*. Even beginners can control their skis after they have learned the wedge (snowplow) turn. The U.S. Ski Association, National Ski Areas Association, Ski Industries America, Professional Ski Instructors of America, and the National Ski Patrol System have devised an eight-point "National Skier's Responsibility" which covers some of the above items and which bears repeating. Here it is:

1. All skiers shall ski under control. Control shall mean in such a manner that you can stop or avoid other skiers.
2. When skiing downhill and overtaking another skier, you must avoid the skier below you.
3. Skiers approaching each other on opposite traverses pass to the right.
4. You must not stop where you obstruct a trail or are not visible from above.
5. When entering a trail or slope or starting downhill, yield to other skiers.
6. A standing skier shall check for approaching downhill skiers before starting.
7. All skiers shall wear devices to help prevent runaway skis.
8. Skiers shall keep off closed trails and posted areas and shall observe all traffic signs and other regulations as prescribed by the ski area.

Lastly, skiers on both sides of the Atlantic can profit from "The Laws of the Piste," which were written by attorneys of the FIS (Federation Internationale de Ski). Here is an extract of a few pertinent legal points, on which European attorneys may base their lawsuits in case of injuries.

- At piste crossings that involve T-bars or other such ski lifts, the law favors the lift user.
- At crossings between pistes and public roads, the road user has the right of way.
- In choosing a piste, skiers must take their own abilities into consideration.
- The skier must watch the signs posted at downhill pistes.
- All parties involved in an accident are obligated to stop to identify themselves and, if necessary, to render aid.

HOW NOT TO BREAK A LEG

Famous cartoon: A skier sits on the lift. He is followed by two first-aid types. The two ski patrollers carry a rescue toboggan, just in case. Another cartoon: The man in the business suit says to the fellow wearing the cast: "I sure like skiing. Some day I really plan to try it."

Skiing isn't as dangerous as it sounds; only about 4 in 1000 skiers wind up on a rescue toboggan per day, and not necessarily with a fracture (sprains are common). Skiing is safer than boxing, football, or ice hockey. And thanks to better equipment and better groomed slopes, the accident figures of the eighties are lower than those of the fifties.

All the same, you should be aware of the possible dangers. When you buy your lift ticket, you're informed (cigarette-package style) about them. The typical ticket warns:

> "The purchaser understands that skiing is a hazardous sport. The purchaser recognizes dangerous conditions may exist, whether marked or unmarked. Falls and collisions are common, and injuries can result, and purchaser accepts the negligence and carelessness on the part of fellow skiers."

Fortunately, medical researchers *know* why skiers come to harm. Continuing studies made by the National Ski Patrol, the American Academy of Orthopedic Surgeons, and other groups all point to the same accident causes with amazing regularity. Among them:

Cause 1: The hurt skiers were not in good physical condition. One characteristic case concerned a group of young New Yorkers who did calisthenics before the season. When the club discontinued the conditioning exercises, three skiers were immediately hurt.

Solution: An hour's calisthenics a couple of times a week, or better still, 15 minutes of gymnastics a day will shape you up for the slopes. One expert suggests 14 days of 10-minutes sessions. Specifically, you can strengthen your legs with half-knee bends (meaning not all the way down). To improve stomach muscles, sit-ups are good. You can also try duck-style waddling – forward, backward, right and left, with hands on hips. Some skiers prefer cycling in autumn to develop leg strength. Don't expect to get into condition *on* a skiing vacation. You have to do it before. (See Chapter 6.)

Cause 2: The skiers use the wrong equipment. A Montana youth of 13 tried his father's over-long skis, but his young legs couldn't manage the length and weight of Daddy's gear. The boy fell, spraining his ankle. Other skiers don't check their release bindings for weeks. The mechanism opens when it shouldn't or doesn't open when it should.

Solution: Have your bindings installed by a qualified shop. Loose ones cause mishaps. Never trust even the most expensive bindings; top manufacturers warn customers about their product. A typical warning comes from a German firm. "The manufacturer cannot guarantee that a ski binding will prevent injuries under all circumstances. Variations in weather, fatigue of the skier, and other variables make it impossible for any binding to insure absolute safety."

In sub-zero temperatures it is advisable to have a shop check your bindings before you put on your skis. (The mechanism can freeze up enroute to the area, especially if splashed with road slush.) Always be alert after a long car or train or plane trip. You will bear the brunt if the mechanism becomes temporarily inaccurate. For extra safety, the boot and its attachments should not only be free of ice but also of grit and dried mud, which can cause malfunction. You should also have ski brakes to prevent runaway skis. Binding experts remind you that the setting depends on your weight, ability, and strength. Ask a *shop* to help you with a release check. "Never monkey with the release setting yourself," says one binding representative.

Cause 3: The injured skiers are beginners who ventured on difficult slopes before they have the skill to cope with steepness, with ruts, with "moguls," trees, powder snow, or with breakable snow crust. They simply don't look at the markers that explain the grade of difficulties. A unified trail marking system tells you if a run is *easy* (green circle), more difficult (blue square), or very difficult (black diamond).

Solution: Study a ski area map beforehand. Watch the signs as indicated above.

Cause 4: The skiers are overconfident. They lose control and crash at high speed. To illustrate, a Colorado sports writer had been a cautious skier for 30 years before he tried to hit 50 mph. The day was sunny, the snow was perfect, and he knew the mountain. But he tried to imitate the racers whom he'd interviewed. He made it to the valley in three minutes. Then he "crashed and burned." His overconfidence cost him a complicated leg operation and eight months on crutches.

Solution: Use common sense. Avoid skiing beyond your ability. High speeds are for downhill racers or experts. Always ski under control. Every skier hates the inconsiderate and selfish person who charges downhill like a bullet, regardless of others, or who crashes his way through a class, or who displaces a slower person on a narrow trail. Remember, too, that "schussboomers" or "bombers" lose their lift privileges at most ski resorts. At some, reckless skiers can even be *fined* or incarcerated.

Cause 5: The skier overdoes it. He goes out too early in the morning (with too little sleep) or stays on the slopes too late. The day's last, wobbly run then causes his downfall. Don't take a chance with fatigue or cold, stiff limbs, or an empty stomach. Lack of food means poor reflexes; tiredness, which the skier often ignores, results in less resilience.

Solution: Don't squeeze every minute out of your ski day. Forget about the cost of your ticket. Stop skiing when your concentration decreases.

Cause 6: According to Dr. Arthur Ellison, a well-known orthopedic surgeon, new skiers sustain injuries because they lack technical competence: "Skiing demands a certain technical capability if we are to pursue the sport safely. It is obvious that the scuba diver would never descend without some knowledge of diving, nor would a potential rock climber take on a hazardous climb with absolutely no knowledge. Unfortunately, we see all too frequently the new skier who puts on equipment which he doesn't understand, takes some lift facility to the top of the mountain and attempts to negotiate his descent without knowledge or technique. . . . The number of *first time* skiers in the first aid room is appalling." The once-a-year skier is in much greater danger than the person who skis regularly.

Solution: Every beginner belongs in a Ski School until he or she acquires the basic concepts of control.

Cause 7: The skiers ski alone instead of in a group. This is a dangerous practice in case of an injury.

Solution: Spend money on lessons. Supervised ski classes are safer. If several people ski together, one person can stay with an injured skier while the other two go for help.

Cause 8: The skiers hit the slope when they're emotionally upset. Psychiatrists' studies show that strong feelings of anger, hatred, bitterness, and other attention-sapping worries cause accidents.

Solution: Ski only when you feel good.

The above list would not be complete without some additional contemporary injury causes. In the high mountains, a newly arrived skier can come to harm because of altitude sickness. That sudden weakness, headache, light headedness, nausea, loss of balance, and labored breathing can be prevented by skiing at the lower elevations first. Then, after a couple of days acclimatization, you can venture up to the 11,000-foot peaks.

Interestingly, too, Dr. H.R. Zick, a well-known researcher, reports that *50 percent of the fatal ski accidents were caused by either drugs or alcohol.* The solution is evident: stay off the strong booze, hash, cocaine, and mind-altering pharmaceuticals.

Here are some final safety points. New skiers often underestimate certain mountain dangers. If you're not properly dressed and are tired and get wet

The ABC's of Ski Lifts and Some Safety Rules   **107**

or cold, you may suffer from exposure, which leads to hypothermia. This condition can result in a dramatic body temperature drop, complete with shivering, sluggish thinking, and even amnesia. Conversely, the hot sun at high altitudes bounces off the snow creating a hazard. Protect yourself against possible snowblindness with a good pair of sunglasses. A reliable sunscreen cream is also recommended.

WHAT TO DO IN CASE OF A SKI ACCIDENT

If you take a bad fall or are injured, don't refuse the ski patrol's help; otherwise, you may seriously aggravate an injury.

Remain as calm and quiet as possible. A ski patroller is on the way!

If you come upon an injured skier, send for help and be sure to give the exact location of the accident. A ski trail usually has a name.

If you are the first person to arrive at an accident, try to keep the victim as warm as possible. Use your parka. Don't move the person. Skis should be crossed vertically in the form of an x above the scene. This warns other skiers and serves as a signal to the patrol. Never attempt to remove the boots of an injured individual, and never give the victim anything to drink. Make sure that the hurt skier has some company.

Members of the National Ski Patrol will soon come to the rescue.

A *patrol searches for avalanche victims with long poles.* (New West Agency).

TEN

Interesting North American Ski Resorts

Skiers always search for a new – and even more perfect – weekend or ski vacation resort. Indeed, the ski aficionado resembles the mountaineer, who must "collect" the greatest number of famous peaks. "Where did you go for Easter?" asks a friend. "Oh," the skier replies nonchalantly, "Sun Valley, Idaho." Or Aspen, Colorado. Or Banff, Alberta. Or any number of U.S. and Canadian meccas.

The celebrated places vary in character, and this chapter gives a brief introduction to more than 30 of the larger and more interesting resorts on this continent.

They're arranged alphabetically. Don't fret if your favorite ski spot is not listed here. It would take several books to describe every North American ski area.

Here, then, is the inside information for the vacationer or the "collector" of famous resorts.

Alta, Utah, is still ideal for those who seek the quiet of gigantic mountains and the thrill of dry powder snow on untracked slopes. (Extensive touring is available, too.) The Wasatch terrain will remind you of the Alps, except for the absence of waiting lines. During the week the many chairlifts yield maximum pleasure. Once an expert-only ski area, Alta can now satisfy everyone, including the most timid individuals.

Alta remains in some respects one of the last of the early American Ski Resorts. This Utah ski niche offers limited lodging and unlimited human contacts; it is among the last bastions for the Real Skier, the person unafraid of steepness, the woman with powder derring-do. Alta is atypcial as American ski places go. It has changed comparatively little in the past 20 years; the frenzy of saloon and discotheque construction has bypassed it. Please remember that there is not a great deal to do here at night. Both food and lodging – American plan – are simple, too. (The most desirable accommodations are at the Alta

Interesting North American Ski Resorts **109**

Lodge.) Less than an hour from Salt Lake City, which is only 26 miles away, Alta is busy on weekends and holidays. It is inexpensive if you just come to ski.

Aspen, Colorado, one of the largest ski complexes in America, was settled by 13 prospectors who invaded the Ute Indian country. The hills yielded some $105 million in silver ore, until prices suddenly plummeted in 1893. A population of 12,000 shrank to 500, and Aspen became another western ghost town. By the mid-thirties, there was life. The first skiers began to filter onto Aspen's slopes after World War II. Thanks to a cultured Chicago financier and some enthusiastic ski instructors, the town struck it rich once more.

Aspen consists of four large, adjacent developments, which carry the names of Aspen Mountain, Aspen Highlands, Buttermilk Mountain and Snowmass. Thus, the concentration of ski facilities is staggering: over 200 miles of skiing from beginner to racer; huge ski schools (more than 300 instructors), lifts by the dozen plus 20,000 acres of untouched snow for touring. Meanwhile, Aspen also proves of advantage to non-skiing groups and families. There is enough to do in town if you *don't* want to ski. For instance, you can sit in the European-style cafes and pastry shops, sun yourself on the balconies and terraces of Aspen's motels, or swim in numerous pools. You can never quite get through all of the restaurants. There are dozens of saunas. At night you can watch torchlight ski descents, foreign movies, and ski movies. The town has some 19,000 beds. It takes about five hours to drive comfortably from Denver to Aspen (210 miles), but there is also a 50-minute, somewhat expensive flight to Aspen's own 8,000-foot-high airport. A train from Denver stops in Glenwood Springs, an hour from Aspen.

Banff, Alberta, has the distinction of possessing one of Canada's largest ski territories, complete with several separate ski areas. A rustic old tourist town (named Banff) provides enough reasonably priced beds in hotels and motels. The huge Banff Springs Hotel, here since 1887, has an old English atmosphere, its turrets and baronial dining areas especially appeal to Americans. This palatial building sticks out from the forest on Banff's outskirts. If you want to get closer to the ski action, select the intimate Sunshine Ski area; it yields excellent vacation possibilities, especially for singles. The beginner and intermediate will find pleasant Alpine terrain here. The Lake Louise Ski Station is Banff's biggest, with lifts and trails reaching hither and thither over several mountains. Gondolas, fast chairlifts, and adequate parking make Lake Louise an important ski center. Fortunately, the crowds from Calgary only materialize on weekends and during the holidays; weekdays are blissful. The same applies almost always to Mt. Norquay, the ski mountain which overlooks Banff itself. The steepness of most Mt. Norquay runs draws racers, hotshots, and eager young bucks from the Canadian provinces.

Bear Valley/Mt. Reba, California, shines with a special gloss composed of white-toothed ski terrain, handsome cedar and redwood ski lodges, and the interesting Californians who ski there. The ski school is excellent, and among the Bear customers you'll see movie people. The Bear charisma extends to the condominiums owned by San Francisco lawyers and their wives and by assorted Los Angeles doctors. Some of the activity leans toward racing, and there are competitions held here every year. Beginners, also, will find adequate slopes.

The area's features include children's ski gear rentals, a "Cub" chairlift, a specialized teaching program for children from four to eight, and special lift rates. The rich fly in from the San Francisco Bay Area in private planes or commercial craft. For the normal motorist, especially one who can't read maps, the approach to Bear is complicated. (Look for "Arnold" on the map.) Most comers stay at least three days.

Big Mountain, Montana, has snow, snow, snow, and skiing, skiing, skiing. Wonderfully uncluttered and nicely isolated, this area works out fine for novices and advanced skiers alike. It doesn't take long to get used to the moderate elevation (5,000 to 7,000 feet) or to the warm, typically western hospitality. Thanks to a lower daily lift rate than elsewhere and some deep-powder runs, you get your money's worth. (Montana just doesn't have any large cities to draw from.)

More than 20 miles of trails and many ski lifts will satisfy all ski appetites. No doubt the dazzling snow formations will strike you: fir, spruce, and larch are as fancily trimmed as wedding cakes, and the Big Mountain Ski Lodge and Chalet seem to be covered at all times with whipped cream. (The snow depth averages 96 inches at Big Mountain.) For especially inexpensive Big Mountain accommodations, stay at the motels in Whitefish, eight miles from the sports activity. Whitefish's location on the western border of the Glacier National Park *doesn't* make it easy to reach from the eastern U.S., but flights to this remote Shangri La come in from the Northwest and California. Some people arrive from Seattle-Portland or St. Paul-Minneapolis by train.

Big Sky, Montana, (accessible via Bozeman, Montana) is another winter resort "sleeper." Big Sky started out with the highest credentials: $24 million from an auto company and an airline. The late Chet Huntley was the prime mover, dynamo, and developer. Located in some of Montana's most rugged and spectacular region, 17 miles from Yellowstone National Park, Big Sky dazzles you with scenery. (It is ideal for long cross-country ski trips and there is gear for rent.) You can reach mountain tops on various ski lifts, in snow vehicles, and via helicopter. Big Sky is an area for conservationists and wilderness devotees. This virgin territory makes for a fine experience.

Most of the Alpine skiing is intended for the average person who derives pleasures from the area's bowls and boulevards, and from the manageable, well-planned runs. Below the cirques, some two dozen interesting runs cascade into the valley, which is almost 2500 feet and several miles under the summit. Some descents measure almost six miles in length. All along, the skier sees the crenelated Spanish Peaks, and on clear days, from some points, you

Interesting North American Ski Resorts

can spot the Grand Tetons. The beginner is taken care of, too, with a special terrain and lift. The area's snow is impressive for its quantity; the storms bring it down from Canada. Big Sky's overall layout is sizeable.

For accommodations there is a large lodge on the premises or write Lone Mountain Guest Ranch, Gallatin Gateway, Montana 59730.

Boyne Mountain and Boyne Highlands, Michigan, claims 120' of snow per season, which isn't astonishing because you're so far north here that you can almost peer into the province of Ontario, Canada. As if this were not enough, the management keeps snow-making machinery on hand to lend Old Man Winter an assist. Still, midwestern skiing has none of the devilish runs which you encounter in the Rockies, and the vertical drop at Boyne (Michigan's highest) is under 500 feet. But the two hills make up for the lack of altitude with building vitality. Boyne Mountain has outdone itself: they have conveyances where *four* skiers can sit together! And there is a special kid's program. Each morning children assemble for ski instruction that continues to noon. Someone then takes the youngsters to lunch in the dining room. Children will reassemble later for afternoon classes which end at four o'clock.

Area accommodations are expensive and include ski lodges. Each room comes with private bath and balconies that look out on the panorama. Some operate on the American plan. The rates include rooms, three meals daily, heated pool, unlimited use of lifts, daily ski instruction, and planned evening recreation.

This area is popular with well-heeled skiers from Michigan, Illinois, Wisconsin, Indiana, Ohio, and Minnesota.

Breckenridge, Colorado, is devoted to a midwestern and eastern clientele. The runs are wide and gentle, making a special appeal to the average North American flatlander. Many vacationers also reach these 9600-foot elevations from coastal cities, both East and West. The snowy terrain is perfect. There is two miles of downhill, which anyone can handle (but is somewhat short for demanding skiers). To spare wind-blown faces and prevent cold noses, the mountain planners sacrificed the 250 feet below the summit. A large maintenance crew spoils old and young by packing and manicuring the Breckenridge slopes. For better skiers, only a few runs offer a challenge. The Breckenridge mountain layout and the signing are simple; no one can get lost here.

Below "Peak #9" you'll notice the tracks of cross-country skis. A complete outfit may be rented locally, and special X-C teachers are available as well. The town offers plenty of condominiums as well as many lodges, motels, and inns. The town itself has a mining heritage and Old West feeling. The hills here are as tame and harmless as the many dogs on Breckenridge's main street. Denver is 80 miles yonder.

Bromley Mountain, Vermont, is one of the East's oldest (1937) and most experienced areas, first recognizing the ski boom after World War II. The mountain looms like a roly-poly lone mini-Matterhorn seven miles east of Manchester on Vt. 11. The top elevation is 3280 feet, the bottom 1950. Double chairlifts with foot rests abound and provide express service to various parts of the mountain. Bromley boasts much snowmaking and sometimes some very cold temperatures.

Bromley caters to young unmarrieds and to families and kids who get special weekday lift rates. A network of trails attracts mostly the beginner to intermediate. The summit of the mountain can provide a five-state view, depending on the weather.

A wide variety of accommodations (for some 2000 persons) is scattered all over the vicinity. Economy-minded skiers go for the "Learn to Ski" and midweek rates at the smaller inns. Good food and good night life are available in the Manchester valley.

Crystal Mountain, Washington, is a deep snow trap. Located 75 miles from Seattle, it is easily accessible to those who are bound for the big city via planes and trains and for those lucky ones who live in Seattle.

The ski resort is marked by the compelling, indelible impact of Mt. Rainier, which has an icy altitude of 14,410 feet. Once you see its glaciated gleaming face, you will not forget it. Rainier is so close to Crystal that you seem to touch the old giant, but you ski on agreeable beginner and intermediate slopes. Crystal also has some of the nation's steepest ski chutes, among them the Exterminator. Snow conditions vary throughout the long season and the natives ski even when it rains.

Instruction is available for all ages, of course, and the resort goes in strongly for junior racing and jumping programs. The area's dining includes two restaurants and the base lodge. You can also lunch on hamburgers atop Crystal Mountain, where the view of various glaciers is outstanding. (It saves you a trip abroad.)

The ski area can be reached by bus and car from the Tacoma and Seattle airports. Before you come, ask Crystal Central Reservations, Crystal Mt., Washington 98022 to fix you up with lodgings. (Things do get difficult on weekends.) All-inclusive five-day packages at this important Pacific Northwest resort go up, like Mt. Rainier, according to the type of accommodation and luxury.

Deer Valley, Utah's most elegant and exclusive resort is just 45 driving minutes from the easy-to-reach Salt Lake City airport. One of the area's summits, Bald Mountain, has an elevation of 9400 feet. Here, you're face to face with 360-degree scenery; there are white-draped ranges in all directions, with wave upon wave of Utah's ski peaks.

Being on private land, the ski area doesn't have to deal with the U.S. Forest Service bureaucracy. Deer Valley thus can build as many lifts as needed. The mountain design offers an excellent mix of terrain for beginners, intermediates, and experts, but the runs are short. Accommodations are long on luxury with commensurate rates.

Interesting North American Ski Resorts

Gore Mountain Ski Center, New York, shows that the Empire State makes some important resort contributions, too. Gore was originally built by experts at the cost of $5 million. Now there are dozens of trails and plenty of lifts that let you glimpse a fine assortment of meadows, lakes, and thick forests. The sleek, architecturally flawless base lodge is perhaps typical for the modern American ski world which "thinks big." There's room here for thousands of cars. A spacious sundeck and a fast-moving cafeteria are also part of the base operation.

Accommodations are available in numerous little towns dotting the region, with thousands of beds to choose from. You'll find this popular ski area south of Lake Placid, which has attracted skiers since the 1932 and 1980 Winter Olympics, and north of the old, rich state capital of Albany. Buses and planes are plentiful.

Despite Gore Mountain Ski Center's location in one of the coldest regions of the Adirondacks, snow is not always plentiful. On the other hand, a gondola ascent can be enthralling for the views of the Adirondack's high peaks and the Green Mountains. Fairly steep faces challenge advanced intermediates, and several wide slopes give the novices plenty of room. Social life is available, mostly in guest ranches and casual small lodges.

Heavenly Valley, California, gives you a beautiful view from 10,000 feet up of blue Lake Tahoe. A passenger tramway takes the skiers to the summit. The area boasts more than two dozen lifts that span a mighty square mileage of skiing. Experts and stronger skiers are slightly favored at this giant area, but there is some territory for the beginner, as well. The ski-complex location (at Stateline) means that you ski in both California and Nevada. There's more: Gambling is allowed in Nevada, and this means casino-subsidized family buffets, smorgasbords, and steak dinners. The South Lake Tahoe township (which comprises the two Statelines) has literally dozens of first-rate motels for less than elsewhere in the U.S. Some hostelries give you free coffee, free TV, and free transportation to the skiing. A word of caution – Heavenly Valley is only cheap if you can stay away from slot machines and gaming tables. Watch some of the big-name entertainers instead. This is a busy town with brassy, noisy Las Vegas touches.

Jackson Hole, Wyoming, has come a long way thanks to its 63-passenger tramway, many chairlifts, and magnificent scenery. Jackson Hole still remains the hotshot's Nirvana, the downhill racer's testing ground, the magnet for the strong-legged. Five-mile descents! Deep untracked snows! Contests for powder skiers! Jackson Hole still has the nation's greatest vertical drop – almost 4200 feet.

Fortunately, during the past years, the resort has added a great number of lifts to access terrain for the less intrepid skier. (The most enjoyable slopes? Look for Casper Bowl.) To some people it may come as a surprise that Jackson Hole also boasts six gentle beginner runs. This doesn't change the total vertical drop or the immensity of this Grand Teton. ("Ski Hosts" and "Ski

Guides" help you get your bearings.) You ski among Engleman spruce, lodgepole pine, Douglas fir, all with their untouched snow covers.

Jackson Hole's scenery is one to match the flora; the Grand Tetons deserve all the famous adjectives – spectacular, imposing, awesome, majestic, stunning. While nature has been handsomely preserved, the town of Jackson (pop. 3000) went through an unexpected development during the past few years. You will spot many new elegant shops, and sleek art galleries flank wooden boardwalks.

The wealthy stay at Teton Village, near the lifts. Economy-minded skiers can room in town at any number of motels that could teach some Colorado resorts a lesson in low prices.

The Jackson Valley is not always easy to get into. A few times each season the planes are unable to land and have to fly on to Salt Lake City instead.

Jay Peak, Vermont, some 85 miles south of Montreal, offers many long lifts. The ski school has an excellent reputation. The vertical rise of 2100 feet is respectable, with lots of terrain for the advanced skier. (For cross-country devotees, there are a number of X-C tours, and there are 80 miles of X-C trails in all.) Jay Peak draws enthusiasts from all over northern New England, as well as from Canada. A tram whisks skiers to the top, offering protection from the sometimes severe Vermont cold spells and winds. And it keeps the ski flow moving. There is also a bit of a boisterous holiday atmosphere at Jay. In fact, Jay Peak's personality is marked by the mix of Canadian and American skiers – all glad to be there and showing it.

After a full day on the slopes, most Alpine skiers retire to homey accommodations in the small towns of Troy and Montgomery Center, huddled near the Peak. Annual Mardi Gras, Easter festivals, and ski school parties are a special part of the Jay Peak aprés-ski scene.

Keystone, Colorado, opened its doors just over a decade ago, immediately receiving accolades for being so close to Denver (75 miles and en route to Aspen), and for being a hospitable intermediate's ski mountain with good management. The vacationer will find a clutch of uphill conveyances at Keystone, plus many miles of trails. About 65 percent of the terrain is devoted to the average skier. You still get the feel of nature in these forests of spruce, lodgepole pine, fir, and balsam; the trail design utilizes the natural glades and dips and curves, so that the aesthetics remain. There is excellent cross-country instruction as well.

The Keystone clientele comes mostly from the eastern U.S. and the Midwest, with a sprinkling from the Canadian plains and Denver. The place to stay is undoubtedly the Keystone Lodge; it has plenty of intimacy, mood, and food for discriminating vacationers. You'll also find condos of all sizes and several motels in the vicinity of the slopes. Keystone is probably the best *designed*, most tasteful resort in the state.

Killington, Vermont, requires the use of an automobile; its ski and lodging facilities are scattered over a wide pleasant area. (If you fly, land at Rut-

Interesting North American Ski Resorts

land, Vt., 16 miles away). Killington actually has six complete mountains, each with its own uphill conveyances, with an hourly lift capacity for 23,000 people. The mountains reach a 3060-foot vertical drop, with numerous difficult trails. There are also some easy ones.

In the base lodges and your ski lodge, as well as on the Killington Hills, you get a feeling of gregariousness. Family business is strong: your children can be placed in a nursery at a daily rate. The small ones can nap while bigger children learn to handle themselves on snow in the special Killington "Children's Ski School." Killington has a good reputation for teaching and instruction for adults is first-rate. (There is a large rental shop in the area, too.)

Mad River Glen, Waitsfield, Vermont, can be reached by plane to Burlington and Montpelier-Barre. (There's also local bus and taxi service.) This old area is proud of its chairlifts and the almost yearly addition of new trails. Mad River Glen is also one of the great boosters of touring, because the developers were always touring addicts. (The Long Trail is one of the X-C favorites, with a distance of about two-and-a-half miles and a descent of 1460 feet.) Better Alpine skiers will be challenged by the Chute and Fall Line runs. Beginners and intermediates find enough activity on more than two dozen trails. A number of double chairlifts serve these slopes and trails.

Mad River is part of the busy Warren-Waitsfield complex where finding bed and board at the last minute can be risky. A recommendation to the discriminating: The Sugarbush Inn in Warren is a distinguished mountain resort in the New England tradition.

The Warren-Waitsfield area offers ample aprés-ski and night activity.

Mammoth Mountain, California, at Mammoth Lakes requires a long drive from Los Angeles, where most of the business comes from. Average motorists who start from Reno, Nevada, will find that they need four hours for the Mammoth trip. Only the most determined San Franciscans attempt it. Nevertheless, the area draws almost a million skiers a year. Why so? The width and breadth of Mammoth's mountains, the massive doses of sunshine, the extra-long season (through June) all contribute to the popularity. On weekends, Mammoth's slopes, cafeterias, and sundecks fetch formidable crowds.

Although older adults are encouraged, Mammoth leans more toward the tanned, handsome college set, especially during vacations, and toward happy-go-lucky bird-free Los Angeles singles. Some of them stay in nearby dorms while others talk their parents into renting a chalet or condominium. Expensive motel lodging can also be available at Mammoth Lakes, the town below the mountain. Night life abounds, including live entertainment. The enormous Mammoth lift network, the versatile ski school, and the slopes are outstanding. The area produced a number of America's top ski racers.

Timberline, Oregon, tops Mt. Hood, the mountainous giant 46 miles from Portland, and also a number of ski developments that attract families. The Mt. Hood ski areas come with cute names like "Hoodoo Ski Bowl" or "Mt. Hood Meadows." Night skiing is one local diversion, and Mt. Hood days

Magnificent scenery can be found at Mt. Hood, Oregon, where you can even ski in summer. (Shorty Wilcox)

can be filled with toboggans and saucers, skating, or hitting the cross-country trail.

Mt. Hood's most renowned lodge and ski mecca is Timberline Lodge. It should only be patronized by crowd lovers on Sunday; smart skiers go there during the week. So much snow can fall on the handsome, timbered Lodge that you're sometimes cut off from the rest of the world for the evening, which guarantees togetherness around the fireplaces. Yet, when the weather is benevolent, skiable Mt. Hood sparkles into view, and you'll be glad you came. Timberline Lodge's ski machinery includes the usual double chairlifts plus several big snow tractors that take skiers and sightseers to the 10,000-foot level for a long downhill run. Above the Lodge, vast open snowfields stretch into — and melt with — the sometimes blue sky. Below the Lodge, tree-lined trails lead to the lower lift terminal or to Government Camp village, a few gentle miles

Interesting North American Ski Resorts **117**

down the mountain, where the night activity goes on. Timberline offers year-round skiing.

Mt. Snow, Vermont, deserves a "Mass Skiing" designation; the area is well "lived in," and everyone connected with it has a long experience in dealing with large groups. Skiers are regaled by a multitude of lifts that criss-cross Mt. Snow, often one topping the other, and running off in all directions. Rocket shapes alternate with countless brightly painted chairlifts. Mt. Snow boasts gigantic, glassed-in warming houses, complicated base lodges, and Japanese Dream Pools, where children can paddle around in hot water amid the plentiful snow. Singles will find plenty of company here; these pools are busy ones. Hotels like the Snow Lake Lodge are a snowball's throw from the mountain. One hostelry features a unique air cable car that carries guests right to the lifts and Main Base Lodge. (Lots of accommodations exist in West Dover, too.)

To cope with an occasional day-attendance of 20,000 people, there exists a nattily dressed ski school staff, who are taught to memorize the skier's first

Mount Snow, Vermont, has always had a reputation for lots of lifts, lots of people.
(Mount Snow, VT)

name within ten minutes. If you want to save money, try the ski week package. It covers five Mount Snow days. The ski resort caters to every type of skier, and the season usually lasts until April or May, when the North Face trails offer excellent spring skiing for the intermediate and the expert. (Mt. Snow is *not* for those seeking intimacy.) You can get here by express bus from N.Y., by Amtrak to Brattleboro, and by air to various other communities.

Mont Tremblant, Quebec, calls itself the "Ski Capital of the North" and spans an entire region within Quebec's Laurentians. Facilities include numerous chairlifts, many miles of trails, ski schools, and ski shops. It is easy to get to Canada's Mont Tremblant region – there's direct air service to Montreal and there are also buses.

You can see the white head of the famous 3100-foot-high mountain from far away. A few minutes later, you'll arrive at the foot of a ski development, which, for its long, varied runs, its excellent uphill transportation, and its lodges, must compare with almost anything in the U.S. More: the Mont Tremblant Company owns hundreds of acres of wooded, meadowed ski land, which still has the same rural, rustic character it had many years ago. (You ski amid maples and birches.)

Lodging suggestions? Try Mont Tremblant Lodge at the base of Mont Tremblant. Gray Rocks Inn at St. Jovite has good accommodations, ambience, and food. There are also special Ski Weeks. If these hostelries are full, you can do as well at several other lodges. You'll also find various cabins and even a little church on the Mt. Tremblant grounds.

Mt. Cranmore, North Conway, New Hampshire, is one of the oldest American ski resorts. It was made famous by none other than old Hannes Schneider, who introduced skiing in the U.S. As a consequence, many old-timers come here year after year along with their offspring. You'll see the customers in the two trams and on chairlifts. North Conway also has everything you need for aprés-skiing.

The typically New England village of North Conway is only a few blocks from the slopes. Despite a 1500-foot vertical drop, the area lacks the ruggedness that attracts the advanced skier. Ninety percent of the trails and slopes cater to the beginner and intermediate.

Park City, Utah, is known as a first-rate ski mecca. Accessibility! You fly to Salt Lake City, board a bus, hire a limousine, or rent a car, then steer toward the snow-free, four-lane super highway, I-80. Turn off onto 224 until you reach the resort – a mere 27 miles in all. And there you are. At your destination, you'll find: 1. a good town with plenty of night life; 2. a great number of lifts; 3. a good-natured mountain. This has the kind of skiing that most vacationers prefer, whether they admit it or not: skiing amid agreeable but not awesome scenery, through groves of aspen and undulating meadows, and along wide, easy three-mile runs. There are no treacherous brinks anywhere, but if you insist, you can swoop down some steep giant slalom hills. Way below

Interesting North American Ski Resorts

and set apart is the vast beginner's domain. Sprinkle it all with top-notch Utah snow, mellow and velvety in the sunshine, and bless it with mining-day names like Payday, Lost Prospector, Silver Queen, the Shaft. You can see why this is a special ski place. For easterners and midwesterners, the skiing must be considered downright ideal. The town's rickety homes grow up the hillside; lodges and hotels alternate with relics of the Gold Rush.

Snowbird, Utah, located just 31 miles from the Salt Lake City International Airport, did things with class and style. First of all, they installed an aerial tramway that carries 125 passengers, plus other lifts. At the same time, Snowbird hired the finest architects to build a stunning 350-bed lodge, a plaza, and shops.

The area employs one of America's best-known ski technicians as ski school director. The mountains are at their most scenic here and the trails, although often steep, are well laid out. This all adds up to: Expensive.

Snowmass, Colorado, offers Alpine width and breadth. The higher you get, the more you realize that these are not the Teton towers or the craggy Sawtooth ranges. Sheer rock is rare around this ski giant, 11 miles from Aspen. Snowmass is more graceful than forbidding, more undulating than rugged.

The village is orderly, compact, and intimate. Lodge buildings stand terrace-fashion, giving a feel of unity. You can step right out of the massive ski lodge and onto the close-by ski lift. Or you can ski down the considerable slopes to Stonebridge Lodge, one among several.

Snowmass has a large array of chair lifts with huge open slopes to ski on. Night life is not as hot here as in Aspen; Snowmass visitors are slightly more sedate.

Squaw Valley, California, is still remembered for the 1960 Olympic Winter Games. Since then, the area has gone through a tremendous amount of refurbishing. Millions of dollars have been spent to satisfy the intermediate skier, too, along with the crack racer. Even the rank beginner is happy here these days. There are now no less than two dozen ski lifts and gondolas and trams to carry you to the peaks and cirques (very busy on weekends). In additon, there is skating, sleigh riding, and swimming, and since many skiers demand a night life, too, you'll find a brisk offering of cocktail parties, fondue parties, ski movie parties, and dancing. Posh accommodations include the Squaw Valley Inn and the Squaw Valley Lodge, with its wall-to-wall carpeting, television, telephone, controlled music, built-in dressing tables and even more luxurious suites. Yet there are reasonably priced motels at Truckee (7 miles, with airport) or at nearby Tahoe City and in the Lake Tahoe vicinity. Reno, Nevada, an important transportation hub, is only 45 miles away.

Stowe, Vermont, is the largest, busiest and best-organized "ski capital" in the East; Stowe's lifts can transport many thousands of skiers to the summits of Mount Mansfield and Spruce Peak. A four-passenger gondola helps, too. Stowe's skiing is considered some of the best in the East. The ski school has excellent instructors; the lodges, hotels, motels, inns, and dorms can handle more than 6000 people, making a longer stay possible for thick or thin wallets. Despite the city-like touch of Stowe's night life, the town has kept some of its early New England character with its white, clean houses, its farms and barns, and a church spire that points to an often cold and snow-laden sky. Stowe has direct bus connections from New York City (323 miles) to nearby Waterbury. Planes land at Montpelier and Burlington, Vt. Stowe has some of the nation's finest ski lodges (a typical one is the von Trapp Lodge) and Inns like the Topnotch or the Stowehof. Although prices are high, so is the quality. Almost 400 acres of slopes exist for every age and every level of ski ability. Stowe has long been a ski-touring center, too.

All these outdoor activities stir the appetite, and in Stowe you can obtain more than just food. You have several gourmet restaurants – some with wine cellars that compare to the best in Europe – with gracious service.

Sugarbush Valley, Vermont, was once known as Vermont's "Mascara Mountain." This four-mountain mass at the summit of the Green Mountain National Forest can be found three miles west of Route 100 and Warren, Vt. A gondola and a number of chairlifts elevate skiers to many slopes containing almost 80 trails. Novices are accommodated, along with intermediates and experts – Castle Rock, Middle Earth, and Spillsville live up to their names. A vertical drop of 2600 feet allows Sugarbush customers to make a three-mile descent. Glamour abounds, but surprisingly enough, some of those Beautiful People and celebrities are good skiers, too.

Accommodations range from the superb (Sugarbush Inn) to the usual condos. The quaint Vermont village of Sugarbush comes with a wide mix of après-ski and supper spots, such as Chez Henri, which offers French cuisine. "Mascara Mountain" guests can conclude the evening at a disco.

Sugar Bowl, California, which first began operating in 1939, is located 190 miles east of San Francisco in the Donner Summit-Donner Lake area. Sugar Bowl features a $1.5 million gondola plus numerous chairlifts that span various bowls, ridges, and runs. Experts and better intermediates are somewhat favored here, although beginners do have some ski terrain of their own. Although the area offers some isolation, the well-known Sugar Bowl Lodge often fills to capacity. The Lodge's rooms and restaurants used to attract mostly San Francisco society, but in recent years, the situation has changed. The lodge offers Tyrolean nights, complete with peasant dancers in lederhosen. The renowned Scarlett Pimpernell dining room, once occupied by Bay Area lawyers in suits and ties, now allows you to appear in a sweater. And ladies need no longer appear in fancy party dresses for the gourmet meals. Prices for lodge accommodations are average. You can sometimes rent a chalet or apartment, or stay in Norden, California.

Lovely snow formations, cold temperatures and a wealthier, more cultured clientele characterize Sugarbush Valley, Vermont.

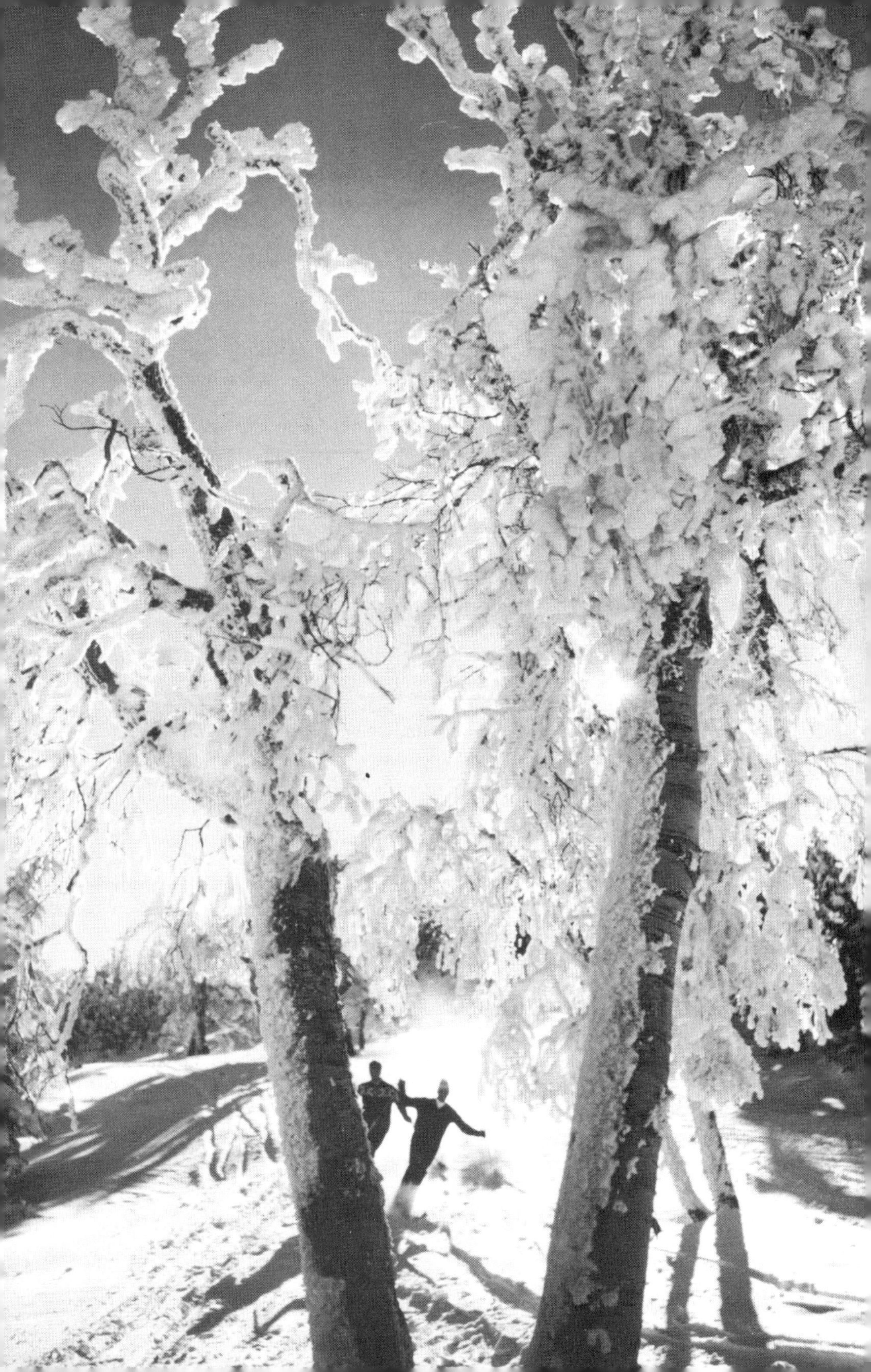

Sun Valley, Idaho, began as an exclusive and posh resort and is still renowned as that, despite many new features. The lodge's room service functions; the Sun Valley cuisine is refined, and any guest can use the two hot-water, open-air swimming pools at no charge. Sun Valley's main street has enforced its no-parking ordinance ever since the resort was built in 1936, and the architects created a no-neon light, Alpine-style village, to which shops and condominiums were added during the passing years. The ski school is one of America's most experienced and largest. Among students and teachers alike, you'll hear many interesting accents.

There are areas which provide easier skiing than Sun Valley's steep, icy Mount Baldy or the short Dollar Mountain. And there are areas with more lifts. (Sun Valley has 14 at present.) But Sun Valley's isolation, its long tradition, and the many extras (giant outdoor ice rink, bowling, sleigh rides, movies, dancing) attract movie stars, producers, tycoons, world leaders, executives, and a young sporty crowd.

Sun Valley itself can be expensive. Accommodations can cost a bundle at the (high-class) Lodge. The weekly bill for a single room or condo is high. A ski shop sells $1500 fur coats, $400 stretch suits. The money-saving solution is to shop and stay in nearby Ketchum. For motel listings, write the Chamber of Commerce. The far-flung resort is somewhat difficult to get to. If you fly in, you must change planes numerous times.

Stratton Mountain, Vermont, is 18 miles away from Manchester, Vt., and, like other New England ski areas, is not especially easy to reach (about six hours to New York). But once you penetrate these deep forests, you're rewarded by a well-groomed mountain, well-maintained lifts, an outstanding ski school, massive snow-making and family doings galore: a nursery for tots ages 6 months and up, Ladies' Day races, Nastar races, kiddies races, Glühwein parties, five o'clock dances, singing by the Ski School, cross-country festivals, Tyrolian folk dancing, and ski movies in the evening. Stratton gets some upper-class customers, and the better lodges are too expensive for the economy skier. On the other hand, there is ample touring for those with modest billfolds and craving for beautiful scenery. A special children's Ski School has its own area, chairlift, and instructors.

Taos Ski Valley, New Mexico, is one of America's most "European" ski resort and a delight to the sophisticated. The nursery has a German name; all the lodges are staffed by Swiss, Austrian, and French chefs; the ski runs call themselves "Lorelei" and "Ruebezahl" and "Mucho Gusto." Taos Ski Valley does an extraordinary job in teaching total beginners, and the vast mountain lends itself to race instruction as well. During the lunch break, some skiers devote themselves to sampling the fancy buffets, to soaking up the New Mexico sunshine, or to resting from the long runs. The air is relaxed, and your hosts are friendlier than at most other ski villages. Your best idea here is the all-inclusive "Taos Learn-to-Ski-Better Week." The best lodges are the Thunderbird and the St. Bernard. (Another is the Edelweiss.) Both stand at the

Taos Ski Valley, New Mexico, is one of America's more sophisticated ski resorts. (Dave Marlow)

bottom of the slopes. The artists' village of Taos is only 20 miles from the ski doings.

Vail, Colorado, is a mecca for the well-off or the powerful. You often hear about Vail's skiing, about Vail's people, and about Vail's shops. The village has spread across the valley, with an abundance of lifts, trails, bowls, and room for 21,000 guests. The "total" American ski resort, Vail is as much a success as St. Moritz, Davos, and Kitzbühel (and just as busy). Vail operates a six-passenger gondola and seemingly countless chairlifts. (A second gondola crashed some years ago.) The ski school is enormous; classiness and high prices are de rigeur for food, lodging, and lift tickets. Vail offers ten square miles of skiing and large open areas for the more demanding Alpine skier. The Vail "Bowls" are justly famous.

Among the many, two good places to stay are The Lodge at Vail (condominiums as well as large rooms) and the Westin Hotel (on Interstate Highway). Do not look for bargains in Vail. Even the Holiday Inn asks for outrageous rates during peak season. This resort isn't for economy skiers or ski bums. Vail's sister village of Beaver Creek is worth visiting for numerous reasons, including reliable skiing.

The Whistler Mountain-Blackcomb, British Columbia, area hides in the Garibaldi Provincial Park, about 75 miles from Vancouver, British Columbia, north of Washington State. As often in the Pacific Northwest, the great lure is scenery. The region is among the world's most spectacular, reminding

Blackcomb-Whistler is one of the more sizable Canadian ski complexes. (Canadian Government Tourist Office)

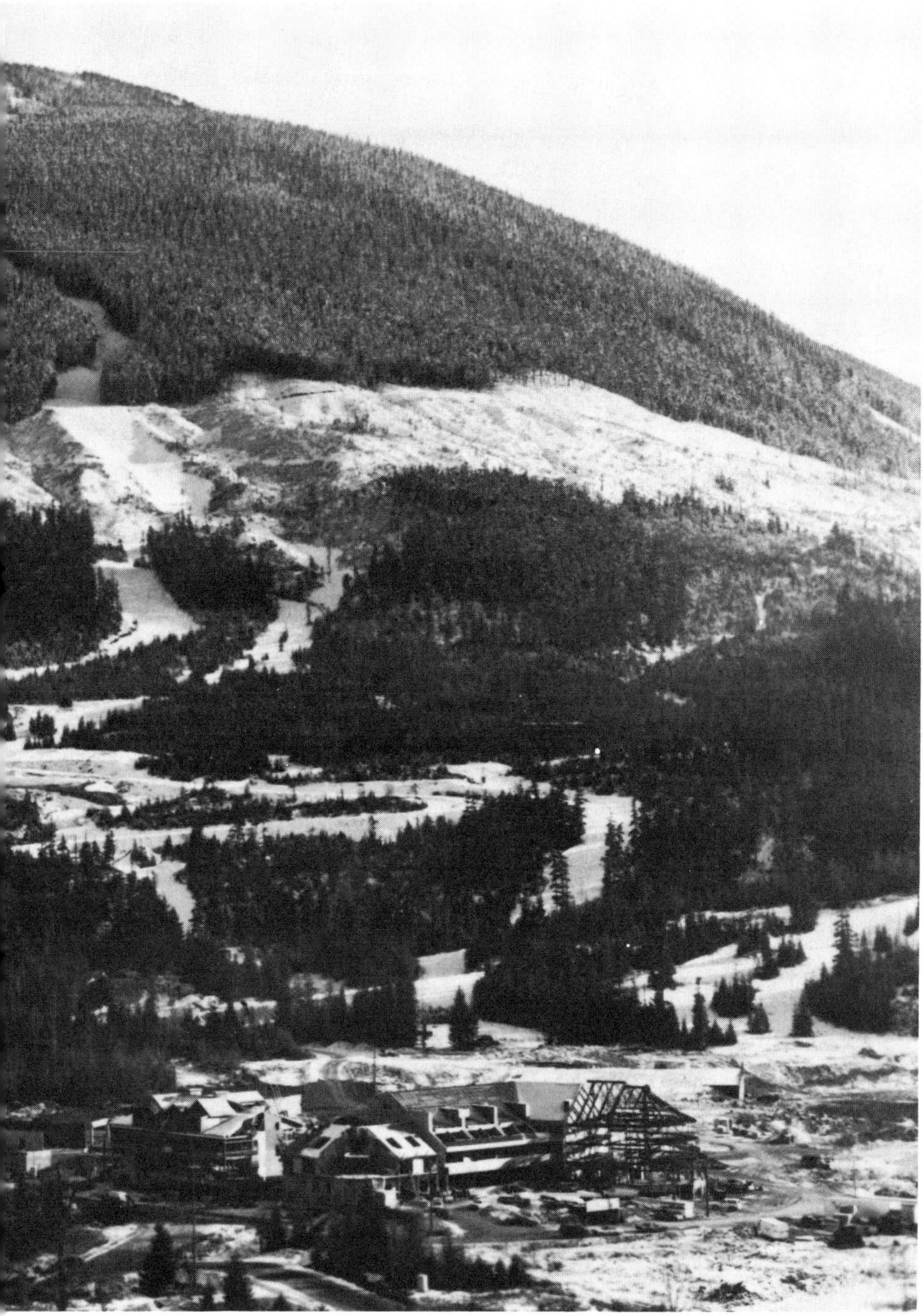

British Columbian areas at Whistler Mountain offer heliocopter skiing. **(Canadian Government Tourist Office)**

you of both Norway and the Swiss Alps. There are giant bowls everywhere, with enormous vertical drops, masses of glaciers agleam in the sun, and expanses reaching all the way to Alaska. No aesthete can resist all those summits and snowfields.

Whistler also has a base village with a few lodges (average U.S. rates). If you come by car, there are several reasonably priced motels. Older persons will welcome the non-taxing low elevations and the myriad cross-country touring possibilities. Whistler's helicopters fly the glaciers at rates that depend on the number of people, number of guides and distance. Choppers make you long remember this Canadian wilderness. Better skiers also get their reward here. Blackcomb, with its 4068-ft. vertical drop, is the new adjacent area, with many triple chairlifts, ski slopes, racing clinics, hotels and restaurants. Recommended!

Winter Park, Colorado, is a popular ski area 67 miles west of Denver. Back in 1937, a Colorado official already predicted: "Denver will surpass the world in snow sports! We have everything here. Scenery and majestic mountains. Sparkling streams. Snow and sun!"

Winter Park long passed the age of 40 and now boasts a big terrain for both Alpine and X-C, a large number of lifts, lots of skiing, and a tradition of catering to the average coast-to-coast Mom, Dad, and kids. Most of the 10,800-ft. mountain unrolls gently. For experts, there is the Mary Jane Mountain. Both southerners (who may have never skied before) and returning midwesterners (who ski once a year) appreciate the well-groomed mountains. Some of the lifts are timed for beginners and the many children. The ski school excels in teaching tiny tots (who have their own tiny hill), and Winter Park has one of the nation's most elaborate nurseries. The adult lift ticket prices are generally slightly *below* the national average for such vast winter sports activities. The resort boasts some 3,500 beds in tidy, cozy, homey inns and in snazzy condo complexes such as Creekside, Beaver Village, and the High Country Haus. Several of the local lodges work on the American plan. Two outstanding ones are Beaver's Lodge and Millers Inn. Both are located two miles from the ski slopes, which are two auto hours west of Denver. Restaurants also abound at Winter Park.

ELEVEN

Where To Ski In Europe

WHY EUROPE: SOME SOUND REASONS

Knowledgeable North American skiers have always been drawn to the Alps; that's where it all began. When Aspen, Colorado, was just an old mining town, skiers were flocking to St. Moritz, Switzerland; Garmisch-Partenkirchen, Germany; or Cortina, Italy. Some of Austria's little villages – St. Anton, for instance – are 700 years old, and ski activity in Norway was brisk three centuries ago. Visit Chamonix, France; you soon realize that the French, like their brethren in the Alpine countries, possess more resort-keeping experience than the still relatively new American ski spas.

Before trilling a love song to the Alps, however, we must say in a most sober voice that Europe's snow is seldom as good as that of the western U.S. or the Canadian Rockies. The traveler should also be warned that he or she must expect more fog, rain, and cold; European weather is less reliable than the blue skies of Colorado. The uphill facilities in Italy, France, and Austria seem old-fashioned by comparison with those in the Rockies. (Even in Switzerland, you still find some Poma lifts, T-bars, and single chairlifts.) At the best Alpine resorts the tramway lines remain horrendous. Prices? In recent years, the dollar bought more on the Continent, with both Americans and Canadians (East Coast variety) being able to save money by skiing in the Alps. But the curve resembles the up and down of the Alps. Hotel rates in France shot up as steeply as Mont Blanc, then plummeted. A quality dinner in most major European resorts still costs a little less than an equivalent meal in the United States. And driving in the Alps makes U.S. interstates a joy compared to the roads of Austria's Arlberg or Switzerland's Engadine regions.

The difference, then, comes in atmosphere, ambience, and overall mood.

European skiing encourages walking as well; footpaths are packed for pedestrians.
(German National Tourist Office)

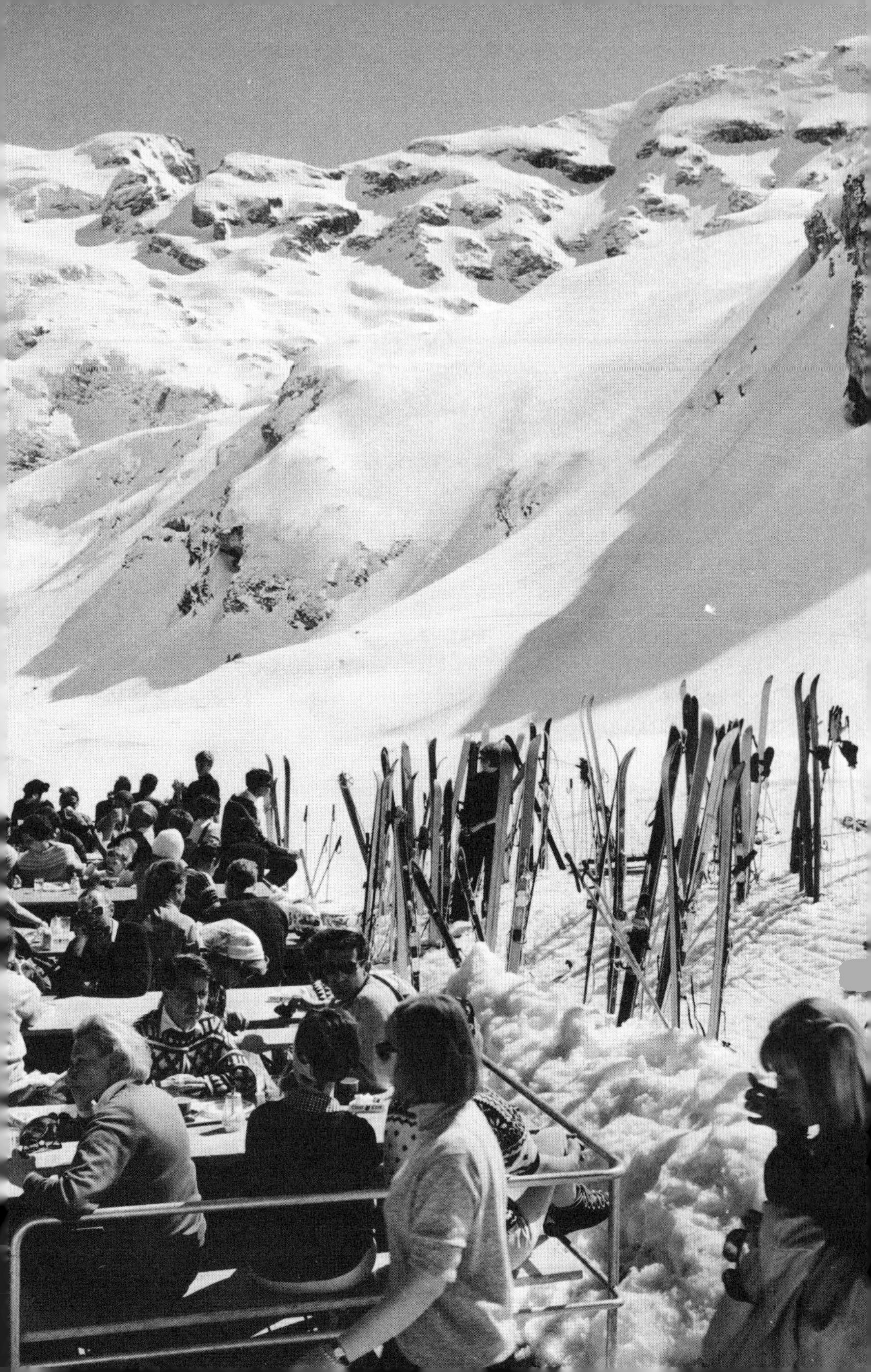

Where To Ski In Europe 131

Even the smallest Alpine hamlet exudes a feeling of warmth and comfort, of *gemuetlichkeit,* of a coziness you'll hardly find in American motels, condo barracks, or skyscraper hotels. The big European resort palaces – say, the Belvedere in Davos, Switzerland – still manage to maintain a personal touch and reflect a classiness and dignity that are difficult (although not impossible) to find in America. European ski lodges ooze with a totally successful get-together spirit and a day-long pursuit of good food. This European passion applies to more than lunch time, when even Vail skiers must content themselves with hamburgers. In the late afternoon pastries are de rigeur all over the Alps, and "tea dancing" or the cocktail hour are still prevalent.

Suppers give the Austrians or Swiss a chance to trot out their local specialties, to let you linger on dish after dish, to sip delicious wine after wine, and to marvel about the excellent breads. Unfriendly as the French may be, the French ski resorts outdo themselves in the meal department. Hors d'oeuvres might be a cold buffet of smoked black ham, chunk tuna, endives, anchovies, sardines. There may follow a splendid fresh fish, accompanied by a light, white dry champagne-like wine, then a meat dish (veal, lamb, beef) with a marvelous red burgundy, then ten kinds of cheeses, topped off with a baba au rum with fresh whipped cream. And all this worship of good cooking takes place in interestingly built, compact ski places in pretty villages. (The beauty of Lech, Austria, or Wengen, Switzerland, is stunning.) American cognoscente also appreciate the cleanliness of Norway, the slowly savored wholesome foods of Sweden, and the peaceful atmosphere of ski places in the French and Spanish Pyrenees.

European skiers still know how to relax. Instead of wolfing down a quick bowl of soup in a base cafeteria, the customers lunch al fresco. They linger in the innumerable outdoor restaurants and cafes scattered over the skiable mountainsides and meadows.

Even the non-ambitious American skier or the non-skier can delight in the menu of an average hotel in the Alps. Here is part of an American plan evening meal from a typical hotel in Garmisch-Partenkirchen, Germany.

Asparagus Soup
Endive Salad Garnished With Eggs and Anchovies
Elk Meat, Stroganoff Style with Fresh Pfifferling Mushrooms
Bavarian Cheeses
Poire Helene
Cafe Espresso
Wine Selection Included

Unlike Americans, Europeans like to sit for long hours in the sun. (Swiss National Tourist Office)

Not even the most enthusiastic European skiers schuss all day long, as some Americans do. Much of the ski time is spent reclining in the sun (with the proper lotion). Vacationers sit and observe other vacationers, or they flirt with each other, or read, or sleep. If you ski in Gstaad, Switzerland, you realize that the Europeans may lounge in deck chairs for hours, getting a tan and marveling at the scenery.

This was always so, and the British who preceded us in the Alps by a century already appreciated what they saw. Milton, Browning, Shelley, Byron and Ruskin all lauded the Alpine landscape. John Tyndall (a physicist and sportsman) grew ecstatic about the Swiss mountains, "Ye splendours!" he wrote more than a hundred years ago. "Can earth elsewhere bring forth a rival?" And indeed, these peaks rise with an incredible massive magnificence from tight valleys to winter-white heights. The resorts are as clean as the Jungfrau glacier. "I must drop everything and travel to Switzerland once more," Mark Twain once admitted. "It is a longing, a deep, strong, tugging longing – "

Swiss hotels are still characterized by their tidiness and, on occasion, by good service. Your hotel room is generally made up when *you* want it, not when it suits the maid. American skiers learn to appreciate the orderly comfortable small pension rooms with their balconies, the cheery little bar downstairs (so different from dark, greasy American taverns), and the spic and span dining areas. This cheer and cleanliness applies to the smaller hostelries in France and Austria as well.

Some North Americans try Europe after they have visited the major resorts in Canada and the U.S. Other travelers return to the Alps because they like the long, long pistes. It can take an intermediate skier a whole afternoon to descend the Vallee Blanche run in Chamonix or the Parsenn in Davos. It is a calming experience to use the lift only once or twice and ski from village to village, as you do in Switzerland, France, and Austria. (Switzerland alone has 200 ski areas!)

TRAVEL TIPS

First of all, plan long, long in advance and study magazine ads, newspaper travel sections, travel guides, airline brochures, and ski magazines. Weigh the pros and cons, and decide only after much thought. Don't let anyone sell you anything until you know all the facts. A travel agent can be of assistance. The agency need not be very large – some small agencies employ people who ski and have been to Europe.

Ask your agent for all-inclusive ski packages or ski weeks. Travel early (December) or late (March and April for high regions) – rates are cheaper then. While the dollar doesn't always buy much abroad, you can wring the most from it by keeping things simple. Avoid the customary error of visiting too many ski stations and seeing too much in too short a time.

Buy a package that limits you to two or perhaps three resorts. Concentrate on these in depth and get to know them well. Keep in mind that: 1) car rentals cost more than trains; 2) airline layovers mean extra charges; 3) so do special bus trips; 4) ski rentals by the week are cheaper than using a new rental shop each day; and 5) many hotel changes mean more tips. Limit your baggage, and travel light; you pay a stiff price to the airlines for exceeding your allowance.

More savings? Ask the travel agent to itemize in advance what you get and have the agent explain a package in detail. Find out whether you're eligible for a special fare. Some airlines often make special rates available. Inquire if lesser-known airlines offer ski deals for the week you want to go. Question your travel agent about the various charter deals. (Make sure that the offerings are on the up-and-up and that the company isn't at the point of collapse.)

Your ski or outdoor club, civic club, or even church may organize ski trips to the Alps at the lowest possible cost. If you're heading to Europe for a professional convention, you can tack on a short ski holiday to your business meetings.

Resorts in the Alps come with plenty of variety and in all price ranges. Here are some of the more interesting ski destinations.

AUSTRIA AND GERMANY

St. Anton-Am-Arlberg remains one of Austria's most picturesque ski villages. The layout is simple enough; the compact main street is composed of solid, massive homes, hotels, pensions, and shops. An array of close-by lifts, all reachable on foot, makes a car superfluous. There is a 3000-foot vertical difference from the immaculate St. Anton roofs to the lofty Valluga Mountain. Endless open skiing possibilities, most of which are ideal for either the strong person or rank beginner, offer less territory for average folks. The Austrian ski system was invented in St. Anton by the late Hannes Schneider and further developed in St. Anton's suburb of St. Christoph by Dr. Kruckenhauser and Dr. Hoppichler. St. Anton has an excellent ski school and superb ski shops (such as English-speaking Jennewein Sports). Visiting weekend crowds from Germany can be a problem because the resort lies directly on an important railroad. St. Anton has plenty of ski racing activity (many racing celebrities hail from here), sleigh riding, skating, and a good ski nursery, all at consistently high prices. Among the places to stay: Sport Hotel St. Anton (well carpeted, well lighted, intimate), Haus Klimmer (a pension). Apartments are available by the week. For dining, many restaurants specialize in elk and deer dishes and mixed grill. (Ski bums eat at Bahnhofs at half that price.) The night life has a cheery, Austrian mood.

Lech-Zürs are two more (lift-connected) Arlberg region villages that make Americans forget the word "plastic." With its 6000 beds, Lech is the larger one and further away from St. Anton. Both Lech and Zuers blend into the treeless

Alpine landscape. The villages give off a warm, natural feeling, yet cater to a sophisticated winter clientele. Zuers gets the Prince of Monaco (and others who welcome the many chairlifts and large ski school). With an almost exclusive devotion to skiing, Zuers forbids snowmobiles, ski bobbing, and has few other winter diversions. Zuers' 2000 beds are occupied by vacationers instead of tourists, and the village is hemmed in. Local owners frown upon growth and generally refuse to sell land to developers.

Lech is five kilometers away, its well-run hotels and clean pensions catering to many habitues who return every year. The attraction is understandable. Lifts sweep up from the scenic village in all directions. At Lech you always ski above timberline, and the many kilometers of trails and bowls offer more escape routes than those of Zuers or St. Anton. Lech's ski terrain is manageable for the intermediate as well. Beginners and families flock to Oberlech, which can be reached by cable car.

Lech boasts one of Austria's oldest (onion-steepled) churches, a quiet river, some "ice bars" on the main street, expensive taxis and fat ladies on horse-drawn sleighs. Like other Alpine resorts (but unlike American ones), Lech tries to remain as it is and sticks to tradition. Among the many Lech hotels, Hotel Kristiania, Hotel Lech (indoor pool, one of several in town), and the classic Haldenhof (with sauna) are of special note. For accommodations in Zuers, try the Central Sport Hotel Edelweiss.

Kitzbühel is a stretched-out metropolis, much like Aspen, Colorado, and Davos, Switzerland. It can be a little crowded because it's so accessible to ski-happy German cities. The crowds have their own good reasons: Kitzbühel has long expert runs such as the Hahnenkamm, the scene of a yearly downhill race, and the magnificent Ehrenbachhoehe. Snow conditions are unreliable because of the low altitude. But in a good winter, Kitzbühel teaches skiing to plenty of people. (Kitzbühel's large school is considered one of Austria's best organized and most advanced.) The resort dazzles Americans with sheer numbers: 55 lifts of various kinds (including many pomas), with an hourly capacity of more than 40,000 persons; almost 100 runs, 9000 beds, countless ex-racers and now-famous sons who operate pensions (among them Toni Sailer), masses of night clubs, and pre-season packages galore. For nonskiers and those who await the not always plentiful snow (altitude: 2700 to 7200 feet), Kitzbühel provides facilities for skating, curling, sleighing, tobogganing, and a big heated indoor swimming pool with Finnish sauna and masseurs. Among the hotel suggestions: Hotel Schloss Lebenberg (an actual castle), Hotel Godener Greif (expensive), and Hotel Jägerwirt (modest). And there are many well-run restaurants. If you do visit Kitzbühel, you might like to take in the stunning old city of Salzburg. (Stay at the Fondachhof, another genuine little castle.)

Innsbruck and environs (pop. 136,000) teem with good ski possibilities ever since the 1964 Olympics were held there. (Innsbruck was also chosen for the 1976 Olympic Winter Games.) The airport of Tyrol's medieval capital is not always open for a landing, so your best alternative is to fly to Zurich, Switzerland, or to Munich, Germany. Rent a car or take a train across the border and you're on your way to the stunning Austrian Arlberg. Twenty minutes from beautifully situated Innsbruck you'll discover Igls, a little village with a tramway and a number of other lifts. Ski the ten-mile long Glungezer run. Try to get into a fairly typical Austrian hostelry like the Parkhotel, Igls. The service is so friendly, so personal, and so kindly that it puts our North American superhotels to shame. The flowers on every table, the cleanliness, and the carefully prepared food all add to your ski pleasure. Apart from skiing, Igls provides dancing, sledding, curling, or simply a quiet winter walk through the lovely valley. Innsbruck is ideal for shopping (at reasonable prices), sightseeing, and steep skiing at the Hafelekar.

Apart from Igls, Innsbruck and its vicinity features three additional places: Seegrube-Hafelekar with tram and several lifts – easy and difficult runs; Mutterer-Alm with several lifts, various ski runs – mostly intermediate; and Axamer Lizum – runs of all grades and a starting point for many interesting tours. These areas have individual ski schools, private guides, and equipment rental. All these ski centers are about 30 minutes away from the center of town.

Innsbruck's old quarter, with its ornate old bistros, handicraft shops, and cozy inns, is the backdrop for outdoor performances by troups of Alpine brass bands and the Innsbruck peasant theatre. Aprés-ski life is brisk along Innsbruck's Maria Theresien Strasse, where you can hear jazz and rock as well as Tyrolian folk music. Good hotels abound in Innsbruck (one example: the Maria Theresia).

Garmisch-Partenkirchen, West Germany, flanks Germany's highest peak, the forbidding Zugspitze Mountain. Various cable cars reach up in every direction; the dazzling Zugspitze itself is connected by a cogwheel train and a spectacular tramway which floats hundreds of feet over the steepest imaginable rocks and over jagged ice masses. The almost vertical tramway cables begin on the edge of the Eibsee (Eib Lake).

A cogwheel train from Eib Lake crawls through many mountain tunnels. (If you want a view, take the tram instead.) The Zugspitze summit is spiked with terraces for sunning yourself (chairs for rent), several restaurants, and a lookout tower from which you can see several countries. White-tipped peaks stretch their heads in all directions. Some visitors like the view so much that they want it for several days, a possibility because of the Schneefernerhaus. This summit hotel has been ingeniously carved out of and built into the massive rocks. Zugspitze skiing takes place at a high altitude but on the unexpectedly gentle and wide slopes of the Zugspitzplatt. The strung-out town of Garmisch (and its other half, Partenkirchen) yield satisfactory ski possibilities to those who came by car or to skiers who can afford expensive taxi rides. (There are buses, but schedules are poor.) Timid skiers should try the Hochalm; intermediates find contentment on the Kreuzwankl. The Kreuzeck-Kandahar is for racers or hotshots. The Garmisch ski school rents equipment (English spoken).

Garmisch has many desirable hostelries. Some hotels feature indoor pools, solariums, gyms, cozy bars, and outstanding dining rooms with meticulous service. You breakfast in full view of the rugged mountains. A few hotel recommendations: the Holiday Inn and the Bernriederhof. Have lunch at the Hochalm.

Hinterzarten, West Germany, is a winter sports resort still to be discovered by North Americans. So far, the Black Forest gets none of the ski crowds you find in the Tyrol or the French Haute Savoie, for instance. Nor do you face the distances of the Alps. Hinterzarten and the Black Forest are quickly reached via Frankfurt or Stuttgart. Hinterzarten's low altitude, about 2900 feet, guarantees a pleasant climate. The ski season is short, however, lasting from about New Year's through early March. On occasion, you can expect fog or rain.

Hinterzarten's chief winter activity is the *Langlauf,* cross-country skiing. The resort also offers a modest Alpine area with a few lifts. And like at all German spas, you see winter hikers; they amble uphill along car-less roads meandering past farm houses. Naturally, you can skate, ride sleighs and sleds, or do a little curling. But the main order of the day is the (Norwegian-style) Black Forest ski tour. Every sports shop here rents equipment. And every surrounding forest has its marked trails; the network adds up to 56 miles. You cross German fairytale forests of fir and spruce while your guide points to the hoof prints of deer and chamois.

Most people appreciate their night's rest. Hinterzarten has about 4000 beds. You can stay in low-priced guest houses, in "gemuetlich" – comfy economy hotels (try the Hotel Imbery) – or the many classier Hinterzarten hostelries. The Park Hotel Adler is the most distinguished one, with a long history of celebrities, a fine bar, some suites, and a gem of a dining room. Even this hotel's continental breakfast is an event, thanks to the local smoked hams, sausages, and cheeses, which the deluxe Park Hotel Adler includes in your room rate.

Mittenwald, Bavaria, attracts expert downhillers with its 2385-meter (7300 foot)-high Karwendel peak; the dramatic giant is reached via a lofty aerial tram. From the Karwendel summit, you not only can see the nearby Zugspitze, Germany's highest, but the Austrian Alps as well. (Innsbruck is actually close by.)

The Karwendel's intimidating Dammkar run is for super-skiers or the super-bold and strong-bodied who must first carry their heavy skis through a narrow 500-meter-long mine shaft. The tunnel opens to a steep snowchute bordered by rock. The Dammkar descent plunges for almost 7 kilometers – a harrowing cannon-shaft of an Alpine run! Luckily for the average person, the resort also built beginner and intermediate areas; these are at the opposite end of town and accessible via a chairlift. Leaving the 4000-foot vertical drop for experts, the milder Kranzberg yields a pleasant *Abfahrt* (descent) across wide meadows flanked by firs, oaks, and bushes.

Mittenwald appeals to the not-so-serious winter vacationer as well. You can admire the town's frescoed medieval houses, and the baroque gilt and gold-filled St. Peter and Paul Church provides magnificent choral and orchestral music. Mittenwald also boasts Germany's only violin museum; the 25 local violin makers are well-known to conductors and soloists around the globe. Certainly, the tourist is apt to gawk at Germany's most rugged mountain chain or inspect the balconied facades of picturesque chalets. Hotels? Check into the spacious Posthotel.

SWITZERLAND

Davos spells bigness, even by U.S. standards. There are 22,000 beds here, three dozen lifts, and 210 marked runs that unspool in every direction. The ski school employs 250 instructors. The town itself stretches for many kilometers, making a car almost mandatory, despite clogged roads. Sophisticated skiers will know that the resort hugs the famous *Parsenn*, a mountain terrain that unravels the Alps' longest runs, allowing you to ski 13 to 20 km over vast, open Alpine meadows, through quiet farm yards, past cafes and restaurants, and through tiny villages. As a rule, you find long lines at peak hours for the Parsenn tramway ascent. Fortunately, there are also some Davos lifts *without* lines. It's just a matter of knowing the mountain layout. The ski fields afford vistas of other nearby resorts, such as Klosters and Arosa. Thanks to a network of mountain trains, you can always get home.

Davos attracts large groups, including many families. These hail from the U.S., Switzerland, Germany, and many other nations. (More than a million people visit per ski season.) Not only an international ski center, Davos is also popular with winter hikers. An enormous rink is available for international figure skating contests (or for all comers), and there's a huge, modern indoor swimming pool, plus curling and winter horseback riding.

The leading Davos hotel is the Grand Hotel Steigerberger Belvedere. This fairly large place has commensurate rates for American-Plan guests. The Belvedere offers the most attractive public rooms in town – special rooms for conversation, writing letters, playing cards, for children, and so on. Room service lives up to the Swiss tradition, and a skier may enjoy the genteel pleasures of pants pressed quickly or the coffee brought up in record time. The Belvedere remains an oasis in an otherwise frequently impersonal resort. The Berghotel Schatzalp (on the mountain) is somewhat cheaper. Modest skiers who don't need private bathtubs naturally obtain the best Davos bargains in various pensions.

Zermatt shares the Grand Central Station moods of Switzerland's larger resorts. All the same, Zermatt still bans automobiles; rapid electric carts or sleighs

Swiss skiing is characterized by long runs past farms and restaurants. (**Müller**)

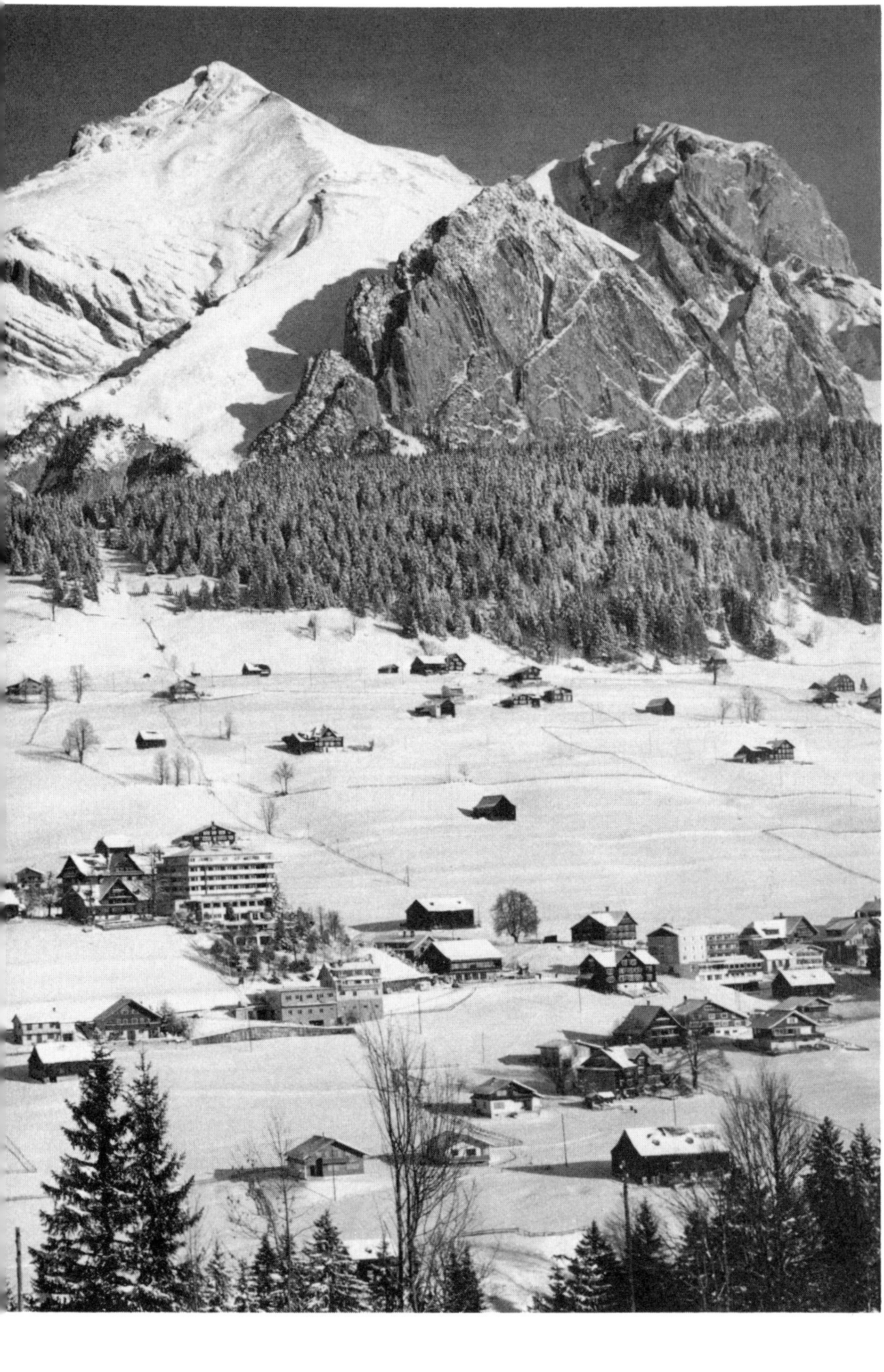

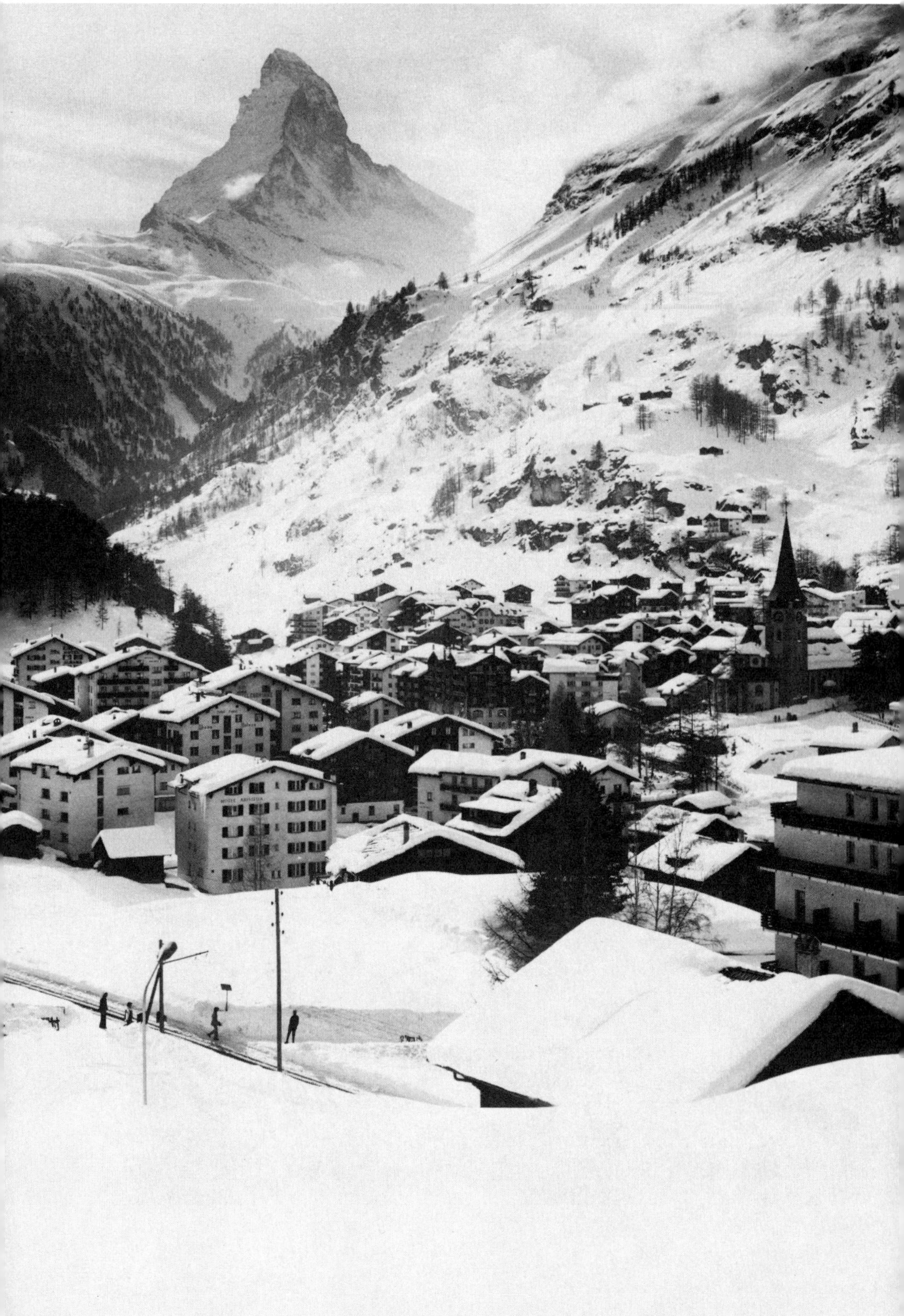

do the job. The triangular Matterhorn draws mainly ski vacationers for long stretches. If you stay a week, you'll soon learn the ski layout. More than two dozen ski lifts and ski trains allow you to roam this immense region. Its five principal mountains, the Gornergrat, the Blauherd, the Stockhorn, the Kleine Matterhorn, and the Schwarzsee provide the kind of terrain that fills every need: steep stuff for the super expert and racer; long, broad expanses for the average person; and lamb-like, treeless hills for beginning skiers. From almost every point, you see the pyramidic Matterhorn. You can ski alongside its broad, sloping base. It is serviced by several lifts (one lift also transports you to Cervinia, Italy). If you have never skied, you might want to try it in Zermatt, which has a long spring season (summer skiing, too). Evenings will draw you to browse through capable Swiss shops.

Among the many good hotels is the Zermatterhof, which is owned by the village itself (good dining, too). Make Zermatt reservations long in advance!

Andermatt, on the massive Gotthard mountain pass, appeals to North American economy skiers, those who don't need deluxe hotels, fancy lifts, or too many compatriots (Andermatt's customers are mostly Swiss or German). A good resort for rugged expert skiers and travelers with modest tastes, this one requires no dressing up or need to bring much tanning lotion. This area is well known for its heavy snows and absence of sunshine.

The ancient town is ringed by enormous mountains, and first impressions stick: Andermatt is old, cold, rugged and rough-hewn, sometimes reminiscent of Alaska, and mostly for skiers and the Swiss Army, which occupies many barracks. (Andermatt traditionally served as Swiss military headquarters.) Here you have long Pomas and steep T-bars. The pistes from Gütsch to Andermatt are varied enough to satisfy many types of skiers for a few days. The cable car to the Gemsstock opens up a more ambitious terrain. In addition to the cable car, there are several lifts, and a seven-day ski ticket for these lifts is a bargain. In addition to teaching beginners and advanced skiers, the ski school has children's classes. A 20-kilometer long piste is open to the cross-country fans. (There is much mountaineering activity in summer.)

The bed count for Andermatt and its neighboring villages is about 1000, including chalet rooms, all at fairly low prices. Even good Andermatt hotels are inexpensive and recommended. Rooms in farm houses can be rented, too. Several good lunch places are scattered over the ski terrain. The mainstay is skiing, but skating and saunas are available. Andermatt's night life proves more lively than you'd expect: rock, pop, waltzes, and combos play for the civilians and for the well-represented Swiss Army.

Gstaad, Switzerland, is always a favorite with the cosmopolitan elite, who appreciate the international atmosphere of the place. Everyone is attracted

Zermatt, with the famed Matterhorn pyramid. (Swiss National Tourist Office)

to Gstaad's outstanding winter sports possibilities. Example? The region has 67 lifts, and a day ticket for all of them costs one third less than Aspen's. Thanks to a location at just 1100 to 3000 meters (3500 to 9900 feet), Gstaad gets some older altitude-wary skiers who don't mind a little wet snow and a lot of sunshine. (The season is longest on the Diableret glacier.) You can also go cross-country skiing all around this world-class resort.

Indeed, Gstaad forgot nothing. There are 100 skiing instructors, several curling coaches, skating pros (for outdoor and indoor facilities), one-hour balloon rides, and helicopter skiing.

Gstaad is easy to reach by train or aero-taxi from Geneva, one of Swissair's gateways. As your electric train approaches the famous winter sports mecca, you quickly realize that Gstaad hasn't capitulated to the building craze of many European communities – no skyscrapers here; no plastics. All buildings – even the local police station, the Olympic indoor pools, condos, and hotels – must be chalet-style, with jutting roofs and honey-colored or brown wood sidings. The architectural unity pleases the eye. You will find chalets scattered up the many alpine meadows. The ski lifts are far apart, so count on spending some money for taxis or waiting for the shuttle buses.

Where should the visitor stay? Surprisingly, Gstaad offers numerous Swiss-clean "garni" rooms with breakfast. But even the small rustic hotels – the 50-bed Rössli or Olden, for instance – charge bargain rates by North American standards. Moreover, Gstaad doesn't get any conventions during the ski season. As a result, even the best hostelries (like the four-star hilltop Grand Hotel Alpina) are as pleasantly quiet as the movie stars' nearby chalets. The best local establishment, The Palace, draws a well-moneyed international clientele.

Laax-Flims, although unknown to North Americans, offers an equivalent of the best Austrian "Ski Circus" – vast alpine terrain interconnected by some 30 ski lifts (mostly tramways and T-bars). Laax's magnificent mountain layout, known as the White Arena, includes the mountains of Flims (which doubles as a summer resort) and the ski possibilities at the village of Falera. Switzerland's largest ski complex can be reached within 90 minutes from Zürich via Chur. You can stay at any number of large hotels in Flims; in Laax, the North American is accommodated best at the Siguine Hotel or a trio with the unlikely names of Happy Rancho, Old Rancho, and Crap Sogh Gion. From there, you can travel to the Vorab (3018 meters). On a good day, the view includes the Piz Bernina, the Piz Palü, and if you're lucky, the Mont Blanc. Unlike most French and Austrian ski areas, Laax offers the pleasures of downhill and cross-country 365 days a year on the Vorab Glacier.

St. Moritz is entitled to its fame as a winter sports center. The famous resort bristles with more than 60 lifts, trains, telepheriques, and cable cars; helicopters stand by at many points and at all daylight hours. Special planes take off for the glaciers; after all, some skiers can't get enough of the easy, tough, mild, harrowing, varied, and immense pistes (which measure 180 kilometers).

The beauty of the Swiss landscape is depicted here, above Wengen. (Swiss National Tourist Office)

This is the Swiss Engadine region and the ski possibilities shine everywhere in and around St. Moritz. The Piz Corvatsch gleams with fields of perpetual snow at high altitude and invites you to ski not only in winter, but also during the summer. A car is useful to reach the widely scattered lifts. Reserve plenty of time to get from one mountain to the next. (Tip: avoid the 10 A.M. rush, no lines at 8:30 A.M.) There is more skiing at Piz Nair (accessible via tram) and from the Diavolezza (summit at 10,000 feet) from where you overlook Italy. With its southern exposure, St. Moritz offers sunshine and many terraces, where you can rest in deck chairs or sit at ice bars. You can skate in six ice arenas or watch international ice hockey games. The world's best figure skaters come to train and give exhibitions. You can curl with famous Canadians. The Cresta Club keeps going strong. St. Moritz still attracts celebrities from around the world, and some of your fellow skiers are either millionaires or movie stars. The prices for chalets, apartments, hotels, and pensions all reflect St. Moritz' stature in the world.

In this metropolis, everyone speaks English, except the French at the Club Mediterranee, which operates a vacation colony in a sizable St. Moritz hotel.

Accommodations? If you can afford true elegance, make reservations much in advance at the deluxe Palace Hotel, which has 300 rooms and twice as many staffers. Carpets stretch everywhere, muffling all sounds. (One bar guide calls the Palace the "Number one resort hotel in the world.") The rates are high, of course. The Carlton Hotel is smaller, and connoisseurs rate it highly, too. Single rates (with breakfast) are again fairly typical for plush accommodations at this famous winter sports spa. The Crystal Hotel is still cheaper, but the parking situation is difficult. The Kulm is slightly removed from the action. Altogether, St. Moritz and environs now have approximately 7000 beds. Rates are somewhat lower after April 15. St. Moritz's shops are expensive but always run with expertise. The town brims with night clubs, cabarets and ballrooms, fashion shows, films, and bridge and chess tournaments. Bring plenty of travelers' checks.

Wengen is a dreamy isolated little resort high above Interlaken, which you can reach by train. From Zurich, you change carriages three times, and the complicated journey keeps out Europe's customary stampede of motorized tourists and day skiers. (The same situation prevails across the valley in Grindelwald, which, like Zermatt, offers no auto access.) Wengen's absence of crowd scenes and the simplicity of the perfect village appeals to seekers of quietness, honeymooners, writers, singles in search of romance, and skiers of all kinds (open terrain). Wengen's altitude guarantees good snow conditions, and the skiing plus the ingeniously linked lifts are superb. You can ski all day long amid impressive scenery without repeating a single run. (Intermediates: try the Maennlichen.) Few Swiss vistas match those above Wengen, where you ski under the indestructible walls and towers of the Eiger, the Moench, and Jungfrau glaciers. Racers use the famous 4,260-meter-long

Where To Ski In Europe

Lauberhorn run, which demands legs of iron; touring skiers can visit the surrounding glaciers.

Airplanes also take off to reach these high peaks. The ski school is outstanding, and ski rentals are available. Because there are no automobiles, Wengen is ideal for hikers who find a network of paths through forests. Everywhere, plateaus and man-made terraces beckon with chairs for sunning. Wengen has provisions for skaters and curlers, and you can swim (indoors) at the Hotel Metropole, a nicely refurbished main street hotel. Among the many other choices, the Hotel Palace will be of interest to an older clientele in search of peace, good service, and fine food. Wengen is a ski place for connoisseurs.

Wildhaus is a slightly offbeat, fairly unknown, and not always snow-rich ski spot for a winter vacation. Few people hear of it except the thrifty Swiss. Wildhaus chalets and hotels stretch in a valley less than two hours out of Zurich. Liechtenstein is about 30 car minutes away. (Train stop: Buchs.) The adequate Wildhaus ski terrain commands a tramway, a funicular, several chairlifts, and T-bars. There is ski instruction, supervised children's skiing, cross-country skiing, curling, and skating.

A whole chalet can be rented by the week, and economical skiers can sleep in nearby farm rooms. For the average person, the best deal is a ski week – six Wildhaus days of meals, lifts, lessons, swimming, bowling, and fondue parties for one price. Don't expect a lot of service, or showers every time; accommodations are also available in the next village of Alt St. Johann. Wildhaus hotels with appropriate names like Alpenblick (Alpine View) or Alpine Rose have private bathrooms. In all, there are 700 beds here. A lift ticket costs much less than at St. Moritz and other celebrated places. At the restaurants, you can dine on chateaubriands, mixed grills, entrecôte steaks, or veal escalopes.

FRANCE AND ITALY

Chamonix remains the giant among French resorts, with room for 20,000 guests right under the nose of Europe's mightiest peak, the 15,700-foot Mont Blanc. This vast ski area encompasses many mountains and many cable cars, a clutch of lifts, long trails (including the Vallee Blanche, down a ten-mile long glacier, and the Haute Route to Zermatt).

During the past 35 years, the Chamonix Valley has undergone an almost complete change, both with its hotel facilities and its structure as a resort. The opening of the Mont Blanc tunnel (seven and one-half miles long) has brought a new aspect to this region, an aspect that the local people could never have foreseen. The tunnel meant easy accessibility of Chamonix and new holiday crowds.

A car is almost essential to get from lift to lift, hotel to bar, ski piste to cafe. As a town, Chamonix provides anything you can think of (and not think of), including an aprés-ski lift that approximates aperitif time in Paris, and a casino,

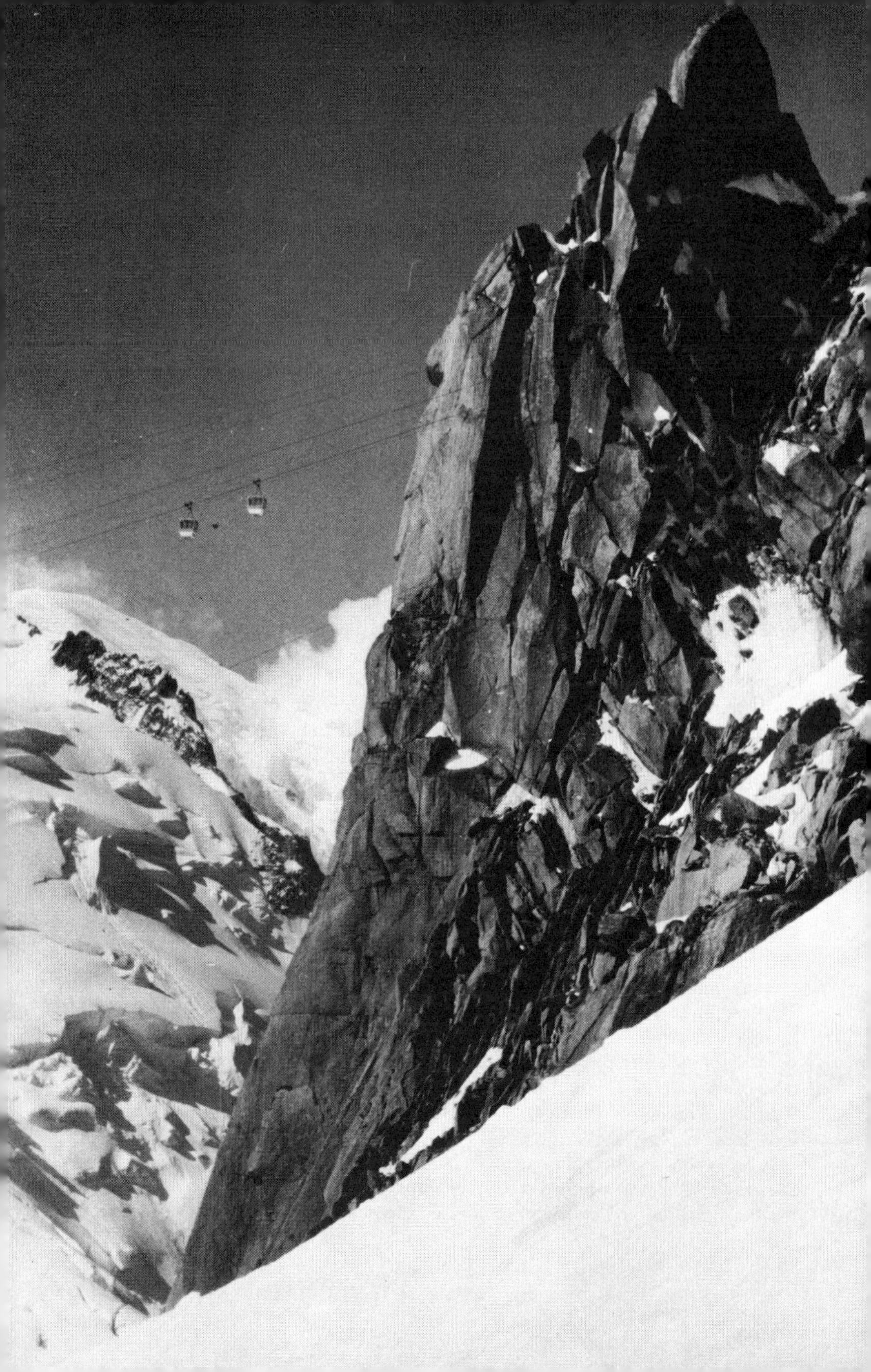

skibob pistes, huge skating facilities, and marvelous restaurants serving fine pâtés, cheeses, wines, and remarkably cooked entrees. Among the hotels, note The Hotel Mont Blanc and Croix Blanche. Chamonix is generally expensive but you can save by buying a "forfait" (ski week) in advance.

You'll find Italy on the other side of the Mont Blanc. The nearest biggest resort is *Courmayeur*. For more Italian super-skiing, consider *Cervinia* or *Cortina d'Ampezzo*. Both can be overrun by hordes of skiers and fur-coated male and female tourists from Milan.

Flaine is a self-contained modernistic skier's island one mile above sea level and about 90 automobile minutes from Geneva. The sun shines often and the wide pistes are devoid of trees. The 15,000 acres of ski terrain, most of it pleasant, treeless, and ego-building, has a 3000-foot vertical drop and enough lifts, including a 60-passenger tramway. For landscape buffs, Flaine can flash one more trump card: a summit view of Mont Blanc, the Alps' highest peak (15,771 feet), and views of many other nearby mountains. The cirque of mountains and the *Desert Blanc* (White Desert) ripple and shine at you around every ski curve, and, at least visually, Americans will be reminded of the powerful Tetons. The Balacha-Les Grandes Platieres and Desert de Plate lift networks feature the greatest number of runs and the longest season. And on the north side of the valley, the Gers-Tete des Verdeta and Veret-Vernant networks are brightened by sunshine. The big passenger tramway and the ski school (yes, a few *moniteurs de ski* always speak English) are definite pluses.

Just minutes away are tasteful boutiques, comfortable bars, and an Emile Allais sports shop. Flaine has small supermarkets that offer delectables and wines for the gourmand. Flaine also has condominium apartments. Hotels include the ultra-modern Les Lindars and Les Grandine Gris. Remember that the best deals for bed, board, and lift tickets go by the name of "forfait." Arrange this in advance with your travel agent or, in bigger cities like Chicago and Los Angeles, at the French Tourist office.

La Plagne, like Flaine, is of comparatively recent vintage, if you compare it to ancient Chamonix. Found 90 miles southeast of Geneva, the resort has several dozen lifts, a long gondola, dozens of French instructors, 80 slopes, and condominium apartments en masse.

The area consists of three ski stations: La Plagne, Plagne-Village, and Aime-La-Plagne. There are numerous hotels and apartment complexes with a total capacity of 18,000 beds. In addition, the ski spa has many restaurants and bars, an auditorium, several movie theatres, ten nightclubs, and shops in an indoor shopping center. The overall atmosphere is typically and animatedly French, with touches of an Anno 2000 ski development on a distant planet.

Cortina, Italy, is that friendly country's best-known resort. It's certainly

---

Chamonix has some of France's most spectacular runs and some of the most unfriendly hosts. (French Government Tourist Office)

a classic one that dates back to pre-World War II days when the first international sports crowd began to flock there from Great Britain, the U.S., and the rest of Europe. Cortina has 60 miles of marked runs, 20 miles of X-C trails, a bobsled run, an ice arena, a huge vertical drop of 6000 feet, a city-like atmosphere (like Davos, Switzerland), and wonderfully cheery hotels such as the Concordia, the Cristallo, and the centrally located Hotel Alaska (yes, Alaska). Cortina is much friendlier than the French resorts, and if you watch your *lire,* somewhat cheaper than France and much cheaper than Switzerland.

Cervinia, Italy, hugs the Aosta Valley, on the warmer side of the famous Matterhorn peak. The ski season here lasts through the end of April. The highest lift reaches almost 12,000 feet and cable cars, gondolas, chairlifts, and even some T-bars zoom off in all mountain directions. For intermediates, the Plateau Rosa is a pleaser with its wide slopes. Racers schuss down from the Plan Maison. Beginners also have many areas hereabouts.

Cervinia excels in nightclub life. Among the newer hotels are the Derby Hotel and the Hotel President.

One final point: Among the thousands of travel agents, only a few specialize in European ski trips. One of the long-time experts is Steve Lohr, at 3 E. 54th St., New York 10022. Another possibility is your nearest Swissair office, which knows the Alps and neighboring countries well.

TWELVE
What Else To Do In Skiland

CROSS-COUNTRY SKIING

Meet a ski guide as he slips out of his log cabin in Summit County, Colorado. He puts on his narrow, feather-light skis and glides off through Engleman spruce forests, past frozen creeks, and along the Blue River.

You join the guide in the valley; you are taken to a trail that meanders gently through meadows, along paths bordered by dignified pines. You hear only the soft purr of the skis and the whisper of the wind in the trees. Occasionally, the guide stops for a look at the gentle curves of the mountains or to examine the tracks of a mink, an ermine, or the snowshoe rabbit. Here is an inexpensive pleasure, a *dolce vita* return to nature, a congenial easy-to-learn sport for all ages. Cross-country skiing, or touring, has experienced an extraordinary rebirth all over the world and especially in the United States. In California alone, for example, some 35,000 persons join the cross-country ranks each winter season.

This Nordic mode of transportation has captured the interest of many Americans who formerly stuck to mechanical lifts at ski resorts. Top professional people now set out on Sunday tours. Students love "X-C" for its simplicity and low cost. And everyone appreciates the lightweight comfortable equipment.

Should you try it? It actually takes little time to become a cross-country addict. The technique is simple, and you need not cope with a single lesson. Ski touring can be limited to flat or gently undulating terrain, which requires neither courage nor a huge effort. Compare it to a gentle winter hike, if you wish, and remember that cross-country skiing is *not* racing or competing. It is recreation. The output of strenght is at first minimal; that is why this activity

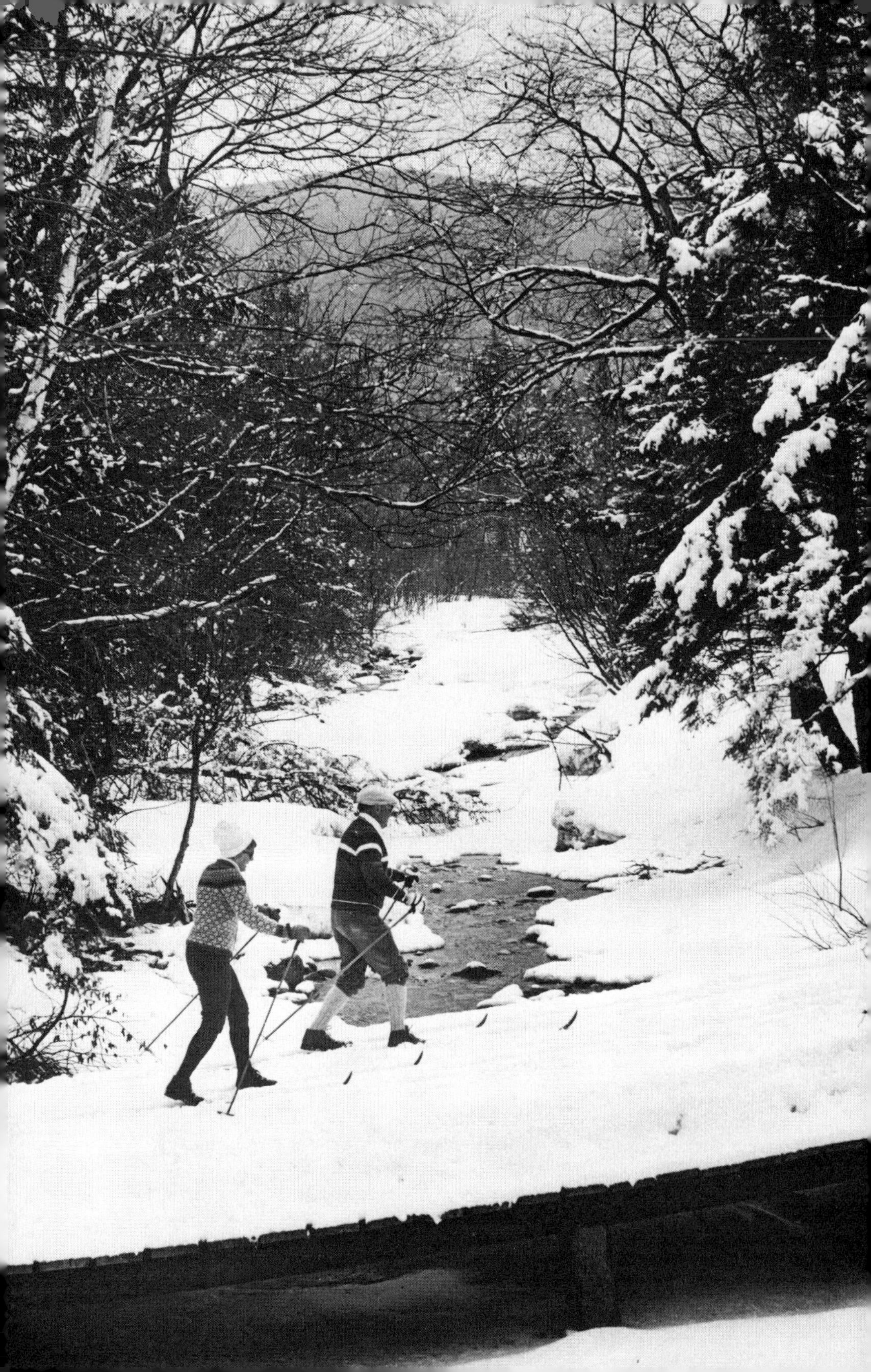

has taken hold among middle-aged men and why children love it. This fast-growing recreation attracts those individualists who are drawn to the quiet, open winter landscape and to the remote forests away from crowds.

Touring is well suited to the "deep" people, the thinkers, the dreamers, the idealists, the conservationists. Many college-age skiers now go touring because they're nature buffs. And they can charge up their lift batteries on an outing with others who feel the same need. By the same token, many older persons find the peace of the ski tour a great health builder. *"Langläufer leben länger"* goes a slogan in the Alps. It means "cross-country skiers live longer."

You will discover that in the era of $22 lift tickets (and long lift lines) ski touring cuts your skiing costs and lets you ski more in a day. Your legs replace the machinery. The sport has become so popular that most ski resorts, especially in New England, employ their own cross-country guides. A modest outlay will get you into the woods with an expert, and a trail fee of a few dollars will let you ski solo.

"The scenic rewards are great," says one typical enthusiast. "All evidence of man is swept under a deep, sound-absorbing blanket of white." Each pine cone and every spruce branch stand out clearly. Nature is always there. "Behind me, the snow was blowing from the peaks; ahead, the sun shone through the trees," a midwesterner wrote in her diary about her first cross-country excursion. You're in Currier & Ives country and grateful for it. What serene silence! What euphoria! Young people's reactions? A group of teenagers were taken into the Sangre de Cristo range, New Mexico. "Some of the boys had never seen a mountain," the guide later said. "It was almost a religious experience to them."

One devotee explains the appeal to adults: "Cross-country is more inner-directed than alpine or downhill skiing," he says. "The rewards and pleasures are from your own experiences and not from the social aspects so common to alpine skiing. Cross-country is an athletic experience. It is self-limiting: you can do a little or a lot, and thus it appeals to city people as well."

Many states provide special trails, or you may want to try your first slides on the local golf course. You can drive to a winter-deserted city park for first outings and later in the season make a cross-country ski trip to a vantage point outside your city. Logging roads, seasonally-closed secondary roads, winter-shrouded jeep roads, and hiking trails offer possibilities for tours; or if you have no access to forests and mountains, you can consider meadows, hills, and fields for touring.

It is fortunate that America's ski areas add touring trails to their general layout. You'll also find that the larger Canadian resorts in British Columbia, Alberta, and Quebec all offer X-C skiing. Some U.S. ski areas with special touring facilities include Snowmass, and Keystone, Colorado; Gore Mountain, Lake

Cross-country skiing appeals to all ages. (Eaton, Waterville Valley, NH)

Placid, and Pound Ridge Reservation, New York; Woodstock Touring Center, Woodstock, and Putney, Vermont; Mount Rainier National Park, Washingtin; and Heavenly Valley, Lake Tahoe, California.

A U.S. ski official adds, "There is no limit to the places a ski tourer can go. Your season is longer, too. You don't need much snow."

If you avoid steep pitches, "skinny" skiing is easier to learn than its high-speed counterpart. It is almost as easy as walking. And neither parents nor children must be especially fit to set out for a two-mile January trek. (A two-day high-elevation tour is another matter.)

High velocity dangers are absent in X-C, which is much safer than Alpine skiing. You can tour for a lifetime without injury. (According to Steve Rieschl, one of Colorado's cross-country directors, there hasn't been a single broken leg in the thousands of lessons and outings at his ski area.)

TOURING TIPS

Rent! Many sporting goods stores and ski shops will let you have everything you need to glide with (and on) for less than the price of dinner. Most ski resorts rent gear, too. When you begin to enjoy the sport — and you will! — you can buy your own equipment.

The touring skier's taste are modest. The beginner's Nordic outfit costs less than the ski rack for your car. And ski touring is hardly clothes oriented. A pair of knickers will do, plus a bargain-table sweater. Since you're away from the après-ski world, you don't need the latest fashions. In fact, you can tour in any clothes that keep out the snow, yet are light enough. Long woolen or fishnet underwear, a wool or flannel shirt, one pair each of light and heavy socks, lined mittens of a waterproof material, a cap that fits over your ears, and a long loose jacket with hood or an old windbreaker make up some of the basic winter clothes. (Very cold regions may require more.) Some skiers put an extra shirt and sweater in their rucksack for longer journeys. In the mountains, the weather can change fast, and extra clothing comes in handy.

Skis for touring should be light and have lift. The lightest and most lively of all Nordic skis is the cross-country racing ski in which light weight is achieved at the price of only moderate strength and durability. The touring ski uses stronger synthetics and is slightly wider than the racing ski. (Almost all X-C skis are now made of synthetics or sandwiches of various materials.) Cross-country skis are more narrow than regular skis and lack steel edges.

The length of cross-country skis should extend from the floor to the wrist of your upstretched arm. The poles should be modern full-length (up to the armpits, standing on the ground). Short ones involve more hard work when climbing, especially on steep slopes where it is difficult to obtain a good hold.

Your X-C binding must allow complete freedom at the heel. In other words, you must have a binding that lets the back of your foot move up and down. Special cross-country skis come with a reasonably priced Rottefella binding.

Cross-country, or "XC", allows you to find some solitude. (Montana Travel Promotion Unit)

Cross-country skiers wear special lightweight boots that are much more comfortable than normal ski boots, and the most expensive touring shoe costs only a fraction of a regular ski boot.

TECHNIQUE

Since your first cross-country trips should be enjoyable, you should begin by going slowly and easily. Try not to tire yourself. It's no secret that a taut muscle consumes energy and tires; a relaxed muscle rests and stores energy for the next contraction. The inability to relax results in stiff, awkward, and unbalanced skiing, which will soon spoil the pleasure of the tour.

It is worthwhile to take lessons in cross-country technique. Ski areas, ski shops, clubs, and even churches organize clinics. Enroll in a special class and ask the instructor to demonstrate how to use your opposite leg and arm at the same time. (One arm is always forward and upward from the shoulder, and your knees are well bent.) You will learn to walk, to glide, to bend your knees, and to swing your arms.

Other major items:

- The cross-country "kick" lives up to its name; you kick one ski backward, which allows your other bent leg and ski to glide forward. The thrust of your back foot makes for excellent locomotion; besides, while your right foot does the work, the left one can rest and relax. Then you switch: you kick with the left leg and slide forward on the right. Your body weight is always on the sliding ski. The technique works well and is often taught without ski poles; this way you can concentrate at first on the footwork.

- Diagonal poling always helps to improve your forward stride by means of using opposite arm and leg at the same time. In other words, the left leg and the right pole move forward simultaneously, and then the left ski pole and the right leg slide forward, all in continuous motion. Your instructor will demonstrate this with an impressive rhythm and gusto. Some forward lean helps in the process. Diagonal poling helps in the flat country, and you can utilize it for climbing, too.
- Double poling adds a note of variety if you want to change your speed, give your legs a rest, or scoot down a gentle hill. The words "double poling" indicate that you thrust with both poles at the same time and at the same point in front of you. Your weight should be forward and your shoulders can assist your arms. A short lesson will teach you this technique. It is good for any terrain except a steep uphill pitch.

It is possible that your instructor was born in Scandinavia, and now assists a regular ski school as a specialist. You'll also meet Scandinavian cross-country teachers in weekend or Sunday clinics for all levels of Nordic skiers. After learning the kick and the various poling maneuvers, you'll be taught how to handle very bumpy or deep-snow country, as well as turns. You'll also get an introduction into the science of waxing. Some skis have "steps" that hold you as you go up a hill; these don't need waxes.

You'll eventually be classified as follows. A **novice** is a skier who can ski under good control with a good snow plow turn and be able to safely descend a trail of up to 15 degrees. An **intermediate** is an experienced skier who can negotiate most all trails and has good control on descents up to 30 degrees. An **expert** is the very hardy type who can take any trail at reasonable speed and bushwack through rough country. Such skiers have also learned the telemark, an advanced maneuver.

ONE FINAL X-C NOTE

Cross-country trips require common sense. Expert guides recommend these important four points:

1. Do not ski tour into the wilderness alone.
2. Always know where you are. Bring your maps and compass.
3. Respect the mountains, and know the limits of your ability. It is better to turn back and be safe, than to go on and possibly become a dead hero.
4. Even on short trips be well prepared. Do not forget sunglasses, suntan lotion, chapstick, wind breaker, matches, repair kit, etc.

The telemark turn, once well known to the Scandinavians, has returned to the United States. Instructors now teach it. (Aspen Skiing Company)

SKI-BOBBING

Call it a bike on skis, complete with handlebars for steering and a saddle to sit on. You may go as slowly or as fast as you please. Ski-bobs lend themselves to gentle downhill trips as well as to races. Some daredevils shoot off the knolls on ski-bobs at 60 miles per hour. One ski-bob champion was clocked at 102 mph.

Unlike skiing, you *don't* have to be in physical shape to ride a ski-bob. Second, you don't have to be young. Children fly downhill on these snow bicycles as do very old people. No effort required. And third, you don't have to be rich; ski-bobs can be rented at dozens of European ski areas for a few dollars an hour. (In the U.S., ski-bobs are rare.)

Ski-bobs remain popular in the Alps where 150,000 of these playthings may be in downhill use. These bikes are easy to control, require almost no instruction, and are safe because the rider always has four points of balance. (Skiers have only two points – their feet.) Instead of wheels, the bike-on-snow has a short steering ski in front and a longer one in the rear. The ski-bobber sits on an upholstered seat and has short skis attached to the feet so that balance is constantly maintained. You slow down by digging in your foot claws or, when you get to be expert, by turning. Best of all, falls are rare and harmless, and you're not likely to get hurt. The Austrians say: *"Ski-bob Fahren, Knochen sparen."* Loosely translated, this means: "Ski-bobbing? Bonesaving!"

There are limitations to this sport: 1) a ski-bob only goes downhill; 2) you can't get any genuine exercise on a ski-bob; 3) the bikes are banned at a great percentage of U.S. ski areas; 4) skiers generally don't like them; and 5) American bobbers are badly organized and find it difficult to obtain equipment or information.

SNOWSHOEING

Snowshoes were used in various shapes for 2500 years or more, their origin lost in antiquity. There is evidence of primitive shoes that showed up in Asia, Northern Europe, and the Arctic regions. The snowshoe survived in North America, too. The North American Indians developed these shoes as a means of locomotion to such a degree that modern technology would be hard put to improve the design. The forest Indians found the short broad shoe best for woods and brush because of easier maneuverability. The plains Indians preferred the longer narrower shoe for hunting and tracking the buffalo. Minor variations in these basic designs evolved through the years.

Presently there are several kinds of snowshoes. The Colorado Mountain

Ski-bobbing is more popular in the Alps than in the United States. (Hajek)

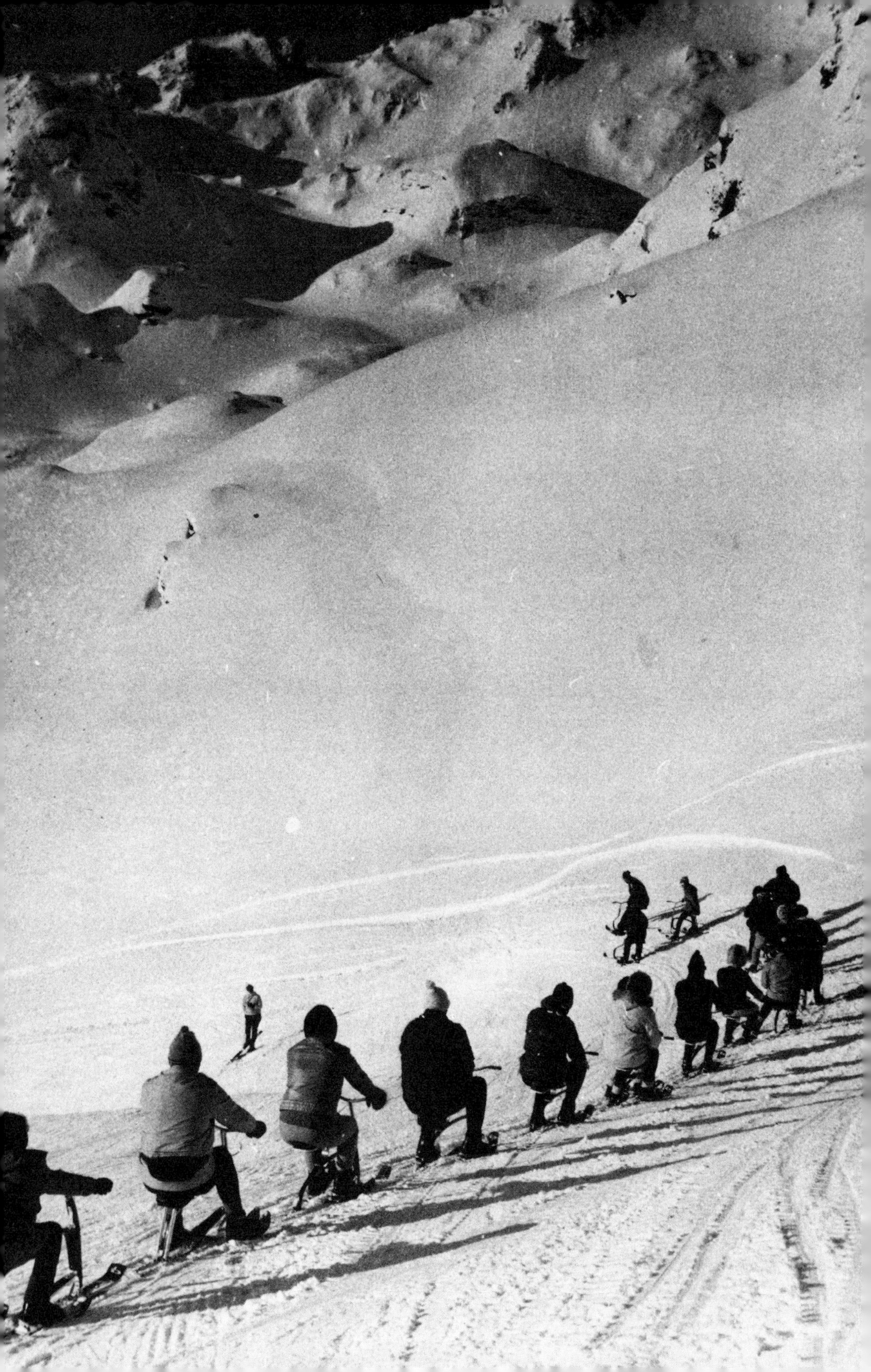

Snowshoeing, an old-new sport, has much in its favor, too. (New York State Department of Commerce)

Club, which organizes winter trips for its 15,000 members, provides the following equipment description:

- Trail Model. For heavy people. Medium width with high upturn 12" x 60".
- Maine or Michigan Snowshoe. Preferred by backpackers or anyone carrying a heavy load because these shoes enable you to hike with your feet close together. Slight upturn to prevent digging into snow. Size desired is determined by hiker's weight and packload.
- Cross-country. This type is 10" x 46", oval-shaped with only a slight upturn at the tip. Toepiece is close to the tip for maneuverability in rabbit country.
- Pickerel (Alaskan, Yukon). Preferred by tall people. Usually 10" x 56" with a high upturned toe designed to clear soft and drifting snow in open country.
- The Bearpaw. No upturn to the tip. The toepiece is close to the front of the snowshoe allowing the mountaineer to step-kick his path up a mountainside. Very maneuverable in dense brush because of its compact size: 13" x 33". No tail.

It's a fairly simple matter to choose a pair. The shape and material may vary, but all of the shoes consist of a frame made of wood, plastic, or metal connected to some lacing. The binding is uncomplicated.

A rawhide shoe is more abrasion resistant and consequently less prone to wear and sagging. Neoprene is a synthetic material which represents a material change in the manufacture of snowshoes. While not as aesthetically appealing as rawhide, neoprene resists snow build-up and is therefore

What Else To Do In Skiland

comparatively lighter than rawhide under wet snow conditions. Neoprene is impervious to gasoline, oil, and rodents and will generally give better wear. You'll also find all-plastic shoes on the market. These work well for people weighing less than 150 pounds. Whatever the snowshoe, no special boots are needed. Hiking, mountaineering, or work boots will do.

These contraptions also serve winter anglers, telephone-line people, utility workers, foresters, zoologists, hunters, and trappers. All can reach snow-blocked areas. A Northeastern family searched for a way to get to their summer cabin on winter weekends. The snowshoe wave caught up with them, and the impossible became possible.

At least in one instance, big business has profited from the great snowshoe comeback. In a small western vacation town, land developers racked their brains how they could make more sales in winter. The housing lots were mostly away from the highway. How could people see the acreage? Unfortunately, few of the elderly customers knew how to ski. One sales person thought of snowmobiles, but many of the conservation-minded prospects objected and wouldn't get on the machines. Walking? The snow depth was often more than ten feet. But a former Canadian suddenly found the answer – he lent his visitors a pair of snowshoes. He took his prospective buyers through a fir forest into the glades which he owned. The land was sold in record time.

Remember that snowshoes can be rented at large sporting goods stores. Stores stock several sizes, and the various models are fine for all strides, including those of children. Even the youngest family members are intrigued by animal tracks in the snow. Experts say that a one mile round-trip suffices at first through the forest or up and down the nearest dales.

The merits of snowshoeing cannot be denied, especially during an era of fuel shortages, air pollution, and inflation. Snowshoes cost little, make no noise, and cause no smog. Snowshoes lend themselves to outings for hikers who don't ski and to people who seek total escape from mechanized ski areas (and even from cross-country trails). You can go anywhere there is snow. Competitively-minded people can even race on them. Winter mountaineers use them to reach the base of higher peaks.

Some final points: Snowshoeing is safe, and snowshoeing is easy enough for all ages. You'll feel awkward at first. It takes a few moments to get used to the shoes. The sport does require some measure of fitness – it is not for people whose main recreation is the television set.

SNOWMOBILES

Snowmobiles look like those electric cars in the amusement parks – only sleeker. The snowmobile has been called a "jeep on skis" or, more modestly, a "motorbike on skis" or a "motorized sled." It is all of these, and can go practically anywhere on snow. Almost anyone can start, steer, and stop a snowmobile. It is that simple.

It should be made clear, however, that these machines do not delight everyone. They pollute the environment. They consume gasoline. They clang and rattle and fill your ears with cylinder explosions. In addition, they demand some mechanical interest; these ski-cars do have starting mechanisms, gears, transmissions, tank-like tracks, and brakes.

The genuine outdoors person will have contempt for a sport which can be done in a sitting position. Conservation-minded people abhor the idea of poisoning the air still further and of invading the wilderness with a machine. (Snowmobiles are known to scare animals.) Some skiers have been so infuriated by the presence of snowmobiles that they have taken the machines apart, making off with parts.

On the other hand, if one sticks to the packed paths, the "sport" demands little expertise and no physical strength. The heavy machine does all the work, accelerating when you want it to, climbing like a docile donkey, roaring over bumps or bridging gaps, and holding its own even on a crooked mountain. Snowmobiles excite motor-happy, gadget-conscious, speed-craving North Americans.

You can ride a snowmobile across a farm field, along snow-blocked country roads, up a logging trail, over a felt-soft meadow to inspect a frozen pond, or straight up a mountain path to a lookout tower. You can reach an otherwise difficult-to-get-to campground and enjoy a winter picnic. Couples fish in winter, thanks to these "jeeps on skis." This Canadian invention also encourages trapping. Some folks utilize their vehicle for birdwatching, winter camping, or just plain trail riding.

Want to try a small outing? Some pointers: Remember that snowmobiles are only in their element when running on *snow*. Your best snowmobiling requires about six to twelve inches of the white stuff, or what might be called a medium snowfall. Extremely hardpacked snow or deep powder, and glare ice, on the other hand, demand trickier handling and require extra driving skill. Compare it to a motorcycle: The more you lean into a turn with your body, the sharper you'll be able to bring the machine around.

Here are a few safety rules given by the manufacturers. Remember that you cannot utilize regular highways. This is forbidden and dangerous because automobile drivers cannot see the too-low snowmobiles. Don't let your children navigate snowmobiles without supervision, and don't allow hotrodding. Finally, make sure your family dresses in thermal underwear, warm undershirts, a good sweater, and a quality parka (down is recommended). Wool caps and leather mittens are essential, too.

AVALANCHES AND OTHER HAZARDS

Cross-country skiers, snowshoers, and snowmobilers all venture off the beaten snow paths of the higher mountains and should therefore know something about avalanches. Here is some elementary information.

What Else To Do In Skiland

- Steepness of slope: The steeper the slope, the more likely the avalanche. However, if conditions are favorable, avalanches can occur on slopes as gentle as 15 degrees, while snow on very steep slopes may not move.
- Shape of slope: Avalanches are more likely to occur on convex slopes than on concave slopes. Most avalanches occur in chutes or couloirs.
- Anchorage of snow to ground surface: The type of terrain has an influence. Rocks, brush, and dense woods hold the snow very well; grass, wet soil, and sparse woods do not.
- Anchorage of snow to lower snow layers: It may take more than a day for a stable bond to form between new snow and the hard or smooth crust of old snow. Before that bond has been established, a dry snow avalanche is likely to occur. If the temperature is high enough for wet snow or for subsequent rain, the snow may become saturated with water.
- Depth of snow: The greater the depth of snow, the more weight must be supported by internal cohesion or by bonding to lower layers, and the more chances of avalanches.

With decades of winter experience behind them, what sort of cold weather advice does the National Ski Patrol have for winter sports enthusiasts? Respect winter for its unpredictable, changeable weather, especially in high mountain country. Dampness and wind are to be reckoned with. Follow these hints:

- To keep out cold, wear several layers of clothing. Wear a good water-repellent windbreaker or parka on the outside. Keep your clothing *clean* and *dry*. Wool socks are best; some prefer a silk sock first, then wool on top. Too much clothing will cause you to perspire.
- Sunburn is a real danger, especially in high mountain country. Sun reflected off snow doubly exposes you to burning. Protect all parts of face, ears, and neck with a good sunburn ointment, especially your lips and nose. Snow blindness is impossible if you wear adequate sun glasses or goggles.
- Frostbite can occur at near-freezing temperatures when high winds are present. Cover frozen parts with dry wool; place frostbitten hands in your armpits. Immersion in lukewarm water is the best remedy. Do not rub frostbitten areas (especially not with snow). Do not subject affected parts to direct heat. Extremities freeze most easily; protect your hands, feet, and face.

Bibliography

A FEW IMPORTANT BOOKS ABOUT THE SKIING EXPERIENCE

Abraham, Horst. *American Teaching Method III.* Boulder, Colorado: Professional Ski Instructors of America, 1982.

Abraham, Horst. *Skiing Right.* San Francisco, CA: Harper & Row, 1984.

Berry, I. William. *The Great North American Ski Book.* New York: Charles Scribner's Sons, 1982.

Berry, I. William. *Kids on Skis.* New York: Charles Scribner's Sons, 1980.

Caldwell, John. *The Cross-Country Ski Book, 7th edition.* Brattleboro, VT: Stephen Greene Press, 1984.

Gallwey, Timothy, and Kriegel, Bob. *Inner Skiing.* New York, NY: Bantam Books, 1981.

Lund, Morton. *Skiing: The Real Skier's Dictionary.* New York, NY: Cornerstone Library, Simon & Schuster, 1983.

Tejada-Flores, Lite. *Backcountry Skiing.* San Francisco, CA: Sierra Club, 1981.

SELECTED TRAVEL GUIDES AND DIRECTORIES

Budget Travel Canada. The Canadian Universities Travel Service. New York, NY: St. Martin's Press, 1984.

Buryn, Ed. *Vagabonding in the U.S.A.* Berkeley, CA: And/Or Press, 1980.

Carlson, Raymond, ed. *National Directory of Budget Motels.* New York, NY: Pilot Books, yearly.

Enzel, Robert. *The White Book of Areas.* Washington, D.C.: Inter-Ski Services Inc., 1983.

Ski Vermont 1984 Winter Guide. Vermont Travel Division, Montpelier, VT, yearly.

PUBLICATIONS

Ski Business
Ski Magazine
Skiing Magazine

Appendix

SOME HELPFUL ORGANIZATIONS

National Collegiate Ski Association
P.O. Box 13123
Milwaukee, Wisconsin 53213-0123

Over the Hill Ski Gang
2530 So. Parker Rd. Suite 204
Aurora, Colorado 80014

Professional Ski Instructors of America
3333 Iris
Boulder, Colorado 80301

Rocky Mountain Ski Instructors Association
P.O. Box 4
Steamboat Springs, Colorado 80477

Rocky Mountain Ski Writers Association
514 Franklin St.
Denver, Colorado 80218

Ski Industries of America
8377-B Greensboro Drive
McLean, Virginia 22102

United States Recreational Ski Association
2901 S. Pullman
Santa Ana, California 92705

United States Ski Association
U.S. Olympic Complex
1750 E. Boulder
Colorado Springs, Colorado 80909

United States Ski Writers Association
2039 S.E. 103rd Drive
Portland, Oregon 97216

REGIONAL SKI ORGANIZATIONS

Colorado Ski Country U.S.A.
Brownleigh Court
1410 Grant Street
Denver, Colorado 80203

New England Vacation Center
630 Fifth Ave.
New York, New York 10020

Ski Areas of New York
6 Parkwood Circle
Box 306
Cortland, New York 13045

Vermont Travel Division
134 State Street
Montpelier, Vermont 05602

Vermont Ski Areas Association
Box 368
Montpelier, Vermont 05602

FOREIGN TOURIST ORGANIZATIONS

Austrian National Tourist Office
545 Fifth Ave.
New York, New York 10017

Canadian Government Office of Tourism
Suite 1160
1 Maritime Plaza
San Francisco, California 94111

French Tourist Office
610 Fifth Ave.
New York, New York 10020

German National Tourist Office
747 Third Ave.
New York, New York 10017

Italian Government Travel Office
630 Fifth Ave.
New York, New York 10111

Swiss National Tourist Office
608 Fifth Ave.
New York, New York 10020

Index

Accidents
  avoiding, 103-107
  what to do if, 107
Air transportation, 42
Alberta, Banff, 109
Alderson, John, 78
Alpenblick, 145
Alpine Rose, 145
Alta Lodge, 108-109
Alta, Utah, 108-109
Am-Alberg, Austria, 133
American Automobile Association, 44
American Teaching Method (ATM), 73-76
American plan, 47
Amtrak, 39-40
Andermatt, Switzerland, 141
Arosa, Switzerland, 137
Aspen Highlands, 109
Aspen Mountain, 109
Aspen, Colorado, 109
Austria
  Innsbruck, 134-135
  Igls, 135
  Kitzbuhel, 134
  Lech-Zurs, 133-134
  Mutterer-Alm, 135
  Seegrube-Hafelekar, 135
  St. Anton-Am-Alberg, 133
Austrian National Ski School, 68
Automobile travel to ski areas, 37-39
Avalanches, 160-161
Axamer Lizum, Austria, 135

Banff, Alberta, 43-44, 109
Banff Springs Hotel, 109
Bavaria, West Germany 136-137
Bear Valley, California, 109-110
Beaver Creek, Colorado, 123
Beaver Village, 127
Beaver's Lodge, 127
Beaver's Village, 6
Beaver's Village Ski Lodge, 45
Berghotel Schatzalp, 137
Bernriederhof, 136
Bibliography, 162
Big Mountain, Montana, 110
Big Mountain Ski Lodge and Chalet, 110
Big Sky, Montana, 110-111
Bindings, 17-18
Black Forest, 136
Blauher, 141

Bolton Valley Resort, 47
Boots, 18-21
Boyne Highlands, Michigan, 111
Boyne Mountain, Michigan, 111
Breckenridge, Colorado, 111
British Columbia, Whistler Mountain-Blackcomb, 123-127
Bromley Mountain, Vermont, 111-112
Bus transportation, 41-42
Buttermilk Mountain, 109

Cable cars, 93, 95
Calgary, Alberta, 43-44
California
  Bear Valley/Mt. Reba, 109-110
  Lake Tahoe, 113
  Mammoth Mountain, 115
  Squaw Valley, 119
  Sugar Bowl, 120
Calories, skiing consumption of, 4
Canada
  Mont Tremblant, 118
  Whistler Mountain-Blackcomb, 123-127
Car pools, for economy transportation, 51
Carlton Hotel, 144
Central Sport Hotel Edelweiss, 134
Cervinia, Italy, 148
Chairlifts, 95, 98
Chamonix, France, 145-147
Chase, Curt, 75
Children, ski lessons for, 66, 76-78
Christies, 86
Climbing, 81
Clothing, 21-24
Colorado
  Aspen, 109
  Breckenridge, 111
  Keystone, 114
  Snowmass, 119
  Vail, 123
  Winter Park, 127
Compression, for parallel turns, 87
Conditioning, pre-season, 60-62
Corn snow, 90
Cortina, Italy, 147-148
Courtesy, skiers, 102-103
Crap Sogh Gion, 142
Creekside, 127
Croix Blanche, 147
Cross-Country skiing, 136, 149-155
Crystal Central Reservations,
112

165

Index

Crystal Hotel, 144
Crystal Mountain, Washington, 112

Davos, Switzerland, 137
Deer Valley, Utah, 112
Derby Hotel, 148
Diavolezza, 144
Dollar Mountain, 122
Donner Summit-Donner Lake, California, 120

Edelweiss, The, 122
Equipment, ski. See Ski equipment
Europe
  skiing in, 128-148
  transportation to, 132-133
European ski vacation packages, 46

Fitness
  for skiing, 58-64
  program for, 63-64
Flaine, France, 147
Fondachhof, 134
France
  Aime-La-Plagne, 147
  Chamonix, 145-147
  Flaine, 147
  La Plagne, 147

Garmisch-Partenkirchen, West Germany, 135-136
Germany, West
  Hinterzarten, 136
  Garmisch-Partenkirchen, 135-136
  Mittenwald, 136-137
Gillingham ski fitness test, 62
Gliding wedge, 84-86
Gondolas, 95
Gore Mountain Ski Center, New York, 113
Gornergrat, 141
Gotthard, 141
Government Camp, 116-117
Graduated Length Method (GLM), 73-76
Grand Hotel Alpina, 142
Grand Hotel Steigerberger Belvedere, 137
Gray Rocks Inn, 118
Grindelwald, Switzerland, 144
Gstaad, Switzerland, 141-142

Haldenhof, 134
Happy Rancho, 142
Haus Klimmer, 133
Health, benefits of skiing for, 3-4
Heavenly Valley, California, 113
Helicopters, 127, 142
Herringbone, 82
High Country Haus, 127
Hinterzarten, West Germany, 136
Hotel Godener Greif, 134
Hotel Imbery, 136
Hotel Jagerwirt, 134
Hotel Kristiania, 134
Hotel Lech, 134
Hotel Mont Blanc, 147
Hotel Palace, 145

Hotel President, 148
Hotel Schloss Lebenberg, 134
Huntley, Chet, 110

Idaho, Sun Valley, 122
Igls, Austria, 135
Innsbruck, Austria, 134-135
Italy
  Cervinia, 148
  Cortina, 147-148

Jackson Hole, Wyoming, 113-114
Jay Peak, Vermont, 114
Jobs, at ski areas, 55-56

Kawendel, 136
Keystone, Colorado, 114
Keystone Lodge, 114
Keystone ski resort, 43
Kick turns, 86
Killington, Vermont, 114-115
Killington Ski Area, 43, 75
Kitzbuhel, Austria, 134
Kleine Matterhorn, 141
Klosters, Switzerland, 137
Kulm, The (hotel), 144

Laax-Flims, Switzerland, 142
Lake Louise Ski Station, 109
Lake Tahoe, 113
"Laws of the Piste," 103
Learning to ski. See Ski techniques
Lech-Zurs, Austria, 133-134
Lifts, See Ski lifts
Lodge at Vail, The, 123
Lodge, The (Sun Valley), 122
Lodges, ski, 5-6
Lone Mountain Guest Ranch, 111

Mad River Glen, Waitsfield, Vermont, 115
Main Base Lodge, 117
Maintenance, ski equipment, 24-25
Mammoth Lakes, California, 115
Mammoth Mountain, California, 115
Mary Jane Mountain, 127
Matterhorn, 141
Metropole, 145
Michigan
  Boyne Highlands, 111
  Boyne Mountain, 111
Millers Inn, 127
Mittenwald, Bavaria, West Germany, 136-137
Modified American plan, 47
Moguls, 88
Mont Blanc, 147
Mont Tremblant, Quebec, 118
Mont Tremblant Lodge, 118
Montana
  Big Mountain, 110
  Big Sky, 110-111
Montgomery Center, Vermont, 114
Mount Baldy, 122
Mt. Cranmore, 118

Index

Mt. Hood, 115-117
Mount Mansfield, 119
Mt. Norquay, 109
Mt. Reba, 109-110
Mt. Snow, 117-118
Mutterer-Alm, Austria, 135

Nevada, Lake Tahoe, 113
New Hampshire
  Mt. Cranmore, 118
  North Conway, 118
New Mexico, Taos Ski Valley, 122-123
New York, Gore Mountain Ski Center, 113
Norden, California, 120
North Conway, New Hampshire, 118
Novice skiers, choosing a ski area for, 26-31

Oberlech, 134
Old Rancho, 142
Oregon
  Mt. Hood, 115-117
  Timberline, 115-117
Organizations, skiing (list), 163-164

Palace Hotel (St. Moritz), 144
Palace, The (Gstaad), 142
Parallel turns, 86-88
Park City, Utah, 118-119
Park Hotel Adler, 136
Parkhotel, 135
Parsenn, 137
Piz Corvatsch, 144
Piz Nair, 144
Plagne, La, France, 147
Plagne-Village, France, 147
Poles, ski, 21
Poma lifts, 101
Professional Ski Instructors of America (PSIA), 67-68
Professionals, ski, 70-72

Quebec, Mont Tremblant, 118

Rentals, of ski equipment, 12, 14
Rope tows, 101

Safety, 103-107
St. Anton-Am-Alberg, Austria, 133
St. Bernard, The, 122
St. Jovite, Quebec, 118
St. Moritz, Switzerland, 142-144
Schneider, Hannes, 133
Schussing, 81-83
Schwarzsee, 141
Seegrube-Hafelekar, Austria, 135
Side slipping, 84
Siguine Hotel, 142
Ski Area Management Magazine, 93
Ski areas
  addresses for information about, 33-36
  checklist for, 31, 33
  for the novice, 26-31
Ski bumming, 51-57
  accommodations for, 56-57

  jobs for, 55-56
Ski clubs, 52
Ski equipment, 12-25
Ski lessons, 65-78
Ski lifts, 91-107
  special rates, 52-53
Ski schools, choosing, 67-73
Ski techniques, 79-90
Ski trains, 39-41
Ski vacations
  packages, 43-46
  packing for, 49-50
  transportation, 37-50
Ski wear. See Clothing
Ski-Bobbing, 156
Skiers, novice. See Novice skiers
Skiing
  advanced, 88-90
  advantages of, 1-9
  disadvantages of, 9-11
  health benefits of, 3-4
  tips for economy, 51-57
Skis
  buying, 14-17
  construction materials for, 16
  length of, 15
  short, as a teaching tool, 73-76
Snow Lake Lodge, 117
Snowbird, Utah, 119
Snowmass, Colorado, 109, 119
Snowmobiles, 159-160
Snowplow. See Gliding wedge
Snowshoeing, 156, 158-159
Spanish Peaks, 110-111
Sport Hotel St. Anton, 133
Spruce Peak, 119
Squaw Valley, California, 119
Squaw Valley Inn, 119
Squaw Valley Lodge, 119
Stockhorn, 141
Stonebridge Lodge, 119
Stowe, Vermont, 119-120
Stowehof, 120
Stratton, Mountain, Vermont, 122
Sugar Bowl, California, 120
Sugar Bowl Lodge, 120
Sugarbush Inn, 115
Sugarbush Valley, Vermont, 120
Sun Valley, Idaho, 122
Swissair, 46
Switzerland
  Andermatt, 141
  Arosa, 137
  Davos, 137
  Grindelwald, 144
  Gstaad, 141-142
  Klosters, 137
  Laax-Flimms, 142
  St. Moritz, 142-144
  Wengen, 144-145
  Wildhaus, 145
  Zermatt, 137, 140-141

T-Bars, 98, 101

Index

Taos Ski Valley, New Mexico, 122-123
Taylor, Cliff, 73-74
Teton Village, 114
Thunderbird, The, 122
Timberline Lodge, 116
Timberline, Oregon, 115-117
Tire chains, 38
Topnotch, 120
Trains. *See* Ski trains
Tramways, 93, 95
Transportation
    to Europe, 132-133
    to ski areas, 37-50
Traversing, 83-84
Troy, Vermont, 114
Turning, 83-90

U.S. Ski Association, 44
Unweighting, for parallel turns, 87
Utah
    Alta, 108-109
    Deer Valley, 112
    Park City, 118-119
    Snowbird, 119

Vail, Colorado, 123
Valluga Mountain, 133
Vermont
    Bromley Mountain, 111-112

Jay Peak, 114
Killington, 114-115
Mad River Glen, 115
Mt. Snow, 117-118
Stowe, 119-120
Stratton Mountain, 122
Sugarbush Valley, 120
von Trapp Lodge, 120

Wagon wheel, 81
Waitsfield, Vermont, 115
Warren, Vermont, 115, 120
Washington, Crystal Mountain, 112
Wedge. *See* Gliding wedge
Wedge christies, 86
Wengen, Switzerland, 144-145
Westin Hotel, 123
Whistler Mountain-Blackcomb, British
    Columbia, 123-127
Whitefish, Montana, 110
Wildhaus, Switzerland, 145
Winter, driving tips, 38-39
Winter Park, Colorado, 6, 45, 127
Wyoming, Jackson Hole, 113-114

Zermatt, Switzerland, 137, 140-141
Zermatterhof, 141
Zugspitze Mountain, Austria, 135
Zurs, Austria, 133-134